RADIONICS
— INTERFACE WITH
THE ETHER-FIELDS

by

David V. Tansley, D.C.

Health Science Press
Bradford, Holsworthy, N. Devon, England

By the same author
RADIONICS AND THE SUBTLE ANATOMY OF MAN

© DAVID V. TANSLEY 1975

ISBN 0 85032 129 8

For my wife

Ellen

ACKNOWLEDGMENTS

I wish to acknowledge with gratitude and to record my sincere thanks to the following for permission to quote from various works:

The Lucis Press: *Treatise on Cosmic Fire, Telepathy and the Etheric Vehicle, A Treatise on White Magic, Esoteric Healing*, all written by Alice A. Bailey. The Agni Yoga Press: *Brotherhood and Aum*. Main Currents in Modern Thought for permission to quote from their September-October issue, Vol. 19, Number 1, and May-June issue, Vol. 24, Number 5.

The British Society of Dowsers: *Principles of Perception in Radiesthesia*. June 1970 issue of the BSD Journal, where it appeared as the winning entry for the Bell Essay Award. The Radionic Association: *What is Radionics?, Radionics and the Electric Patterns of Life and Bio-Dynamic Rhythm*. Neville Spearman: *Blueprint for Immortality* by Dr S. Burr.

Mrs Marjorie de la Warr and the De La Warr Laboratories for permission to quote from *Mind and Matter* and their Newsletter, also for kindly supplying and giving me permission to use two radionic photographs.

I would also like to acknowledge the debt I owe to Mr Malcolm Rae for all the help he has given me; and for his knowledge of radionics, especially in the field of potency simulation which he has generously shared with me, and for permission to quote from his article on *Potency Simulation* which appeared in the March 1973 issue of the Radionic Quarterly. Also for supplying the drawings of the Potency Simulator and Potency Preparer.

My thanks also to Dr and Mrs A. Westlake for the help and encouragement they have given to me over the years, and for permission to use the illustration of the Psionic Chart.

I am also very grateful to Dr Cynthia Drown Chatfield, DC for permission to quote from the writings of her mother Dr Ruth Drown, DC and for so kindly supplying me with the radionic picture of the pineal gland and giving permission for its use in this book.

I would also like to thank my colleagues in The Radionic Association. Their enthusiasm is a constant source of inspiration and especially Miss Elizabeth Baerlein and Mrs Lavender Dower for allowing me to use their radionic photographs.

CONTENTS

LIST OF ILLUSTRATIONS

FOREWORD

It is a great pleasure to write a Foreword to this most opportune of books as it comes at a time when it is evident that a new dimension must be added to medicine if further progress is to be made in understanding the true and fundamental causation of disorder and disease.

During this century modern medical science has explored in depth the physical and material structure and functioning of the human body, right down to the cellular make-up and beyond, to the realm of molecular biology, and the telluric forces which operate. But in spite of this vast knowledge it has made little progress in understanding or detecting what Sir James Mackenzie called 'the predisposing stage of disease', that condition when there is still no damage to tissues or cells and no pathological changes either histological or morphological.

The result of this lack of fundamental knowledge is that modern medicine usually only deals with the disorder when it has advanced into the realm of pathology. At this stage treatment of symptoms is usually all that can be done and this applies particularly to chronic disease – or, in other words, the basic factors causing these pathological changes are largely unknown, and the true nature of health is an enigma.

This state of affairs has given rise to a desire to get down to more fundamental healing, hence the coming of what is called Fringe or Alternative medicine which consists, in the main, of unorthodox therapies which give results but more often than not appear to have no scientific raison d'etre, and thus are not acceptable to orthodox medicine, and yet, especially in chronic disease, yield cures not obtained by orthodox means.

This is particularly true in the more way-out techniques and therapies of Radiesthetic medicine or medical dowsing, and its close ally Radionics, both of which use the supersensible sense – the radiesthetic faculty – to diagnose and heal and deal with pre-disposing states at the root. This can be done, if necessary, at a distance and by remedies which have no material substance in them, only a healing force.

To explain the rationale of such techniques and therapies it is

vii

obvious we must invoke a new dimension, as it cannot be explained in terms of the ordinary data of modern materialistic science, but it can be explained, at least tentatively, if we adopt the hypothesis of a force or life-field called the Etheric – the living formative matrix of cosmic patterns.

This, at present, is largely an unexplored field of study and practice, but the author of this book is a well qualified pioneer to investigate such a field, and in this work he has explored to some good purpose. I think readers will agree that he is an excellent guide in these difficult and largely unfathomed realms, and that although he is dealing with relative intangibles his hypothesies and theories make scientific sense and the Etheric something which is very real and active and cogent in explaining the various phenomena of this new dimension in healing.

As far as I know no book of this nature has yet been written, but I am sure it will be a landmark in the unravelling of these new spiritual – scientific fields of study, which will provide a sound base for further investigation by other seekers after truth and knowledge, and which will, in the end, produce a true integration of the art and science of health and healing.

AUBREY T. WESTLAKE
BA, MB, B Chir., MRCS, LRCP.

WHAT IS RADIONICS?

WHAT IS RADIONICS?

It is a method of healing at a distance through the medium of an instrument or other means using the ESP faculty. In this way, a trained and competent practitioner can discover the cause of disease within a living system, be it human, animal, plant or the soil itself. Suitable therapeutic energies can then be made available to the patient or subject to help to restore optimum health.

THE ORIGINS AND DEVELOPMENT OF RADIONICS

Radionics was originated by a distinguished American physician, Dr Albert Abrams, who was born in San Francisco in 1863. His parents planned that he should complete his education at Balliol College, Oxford, but a visit to Heidelberg made him decide he would prefer to study in the University of that city. From there he graduated with the degree of MD, including first class honours and the gold medal of the University, thus becoming as highly qualified as any physician of his time. In America, Abrams was Professor of Pathology and Director of the Cooper Medical College (Dept. of Medicine, Leland Stanford University of California); he also held the post of President of the San Francisco Medical Chirurgical Society. He wrote several medical text books (one dealing with spinal reflexes ran through five editions in four years) and he eventually won for himself a national reputation as a specialist in diseases of the nervous system.

Abrams, in the course of his research, devised an instrument with calibrated dials which enabled him to measure disease reactions and intensities in his patients. From this work, which Abrams called ERA or the Electronic Reaction of Abrams, came Radionics as we know it today. Abrams' pioneering work attracted much criticism from his fellow practitioners and they sought to discredit him in every way possible. In due course his instruments came to England and in 1924, the year of Abrams' death, a Committee under the

Chairmanship of Sir Thomas (later Lord) Horder investigated his claims. To the astonishment of the medical profession, the Committee had reluctantly to admit, after exhaustive tests had been carefully run, that Abrams' claims about the diagnostic value of his methods were proven. Lord Horder later said, 'The fundamental proposition originally announced by Dr Albert Abrams must be regarded as established to a very high degree of probability.'

Perceptive physicians took up the practice of the Abrams technique, not least amongst them being the late Sir James Barr who wrote a book on the subject of Abrams' work and his great contribution to medicine.

In the United States a Chiropractor named Ruth Drown added further dimensions to Radionics, developing new and more sophisticated instrumentation and new diagnostic and treatment techniques. In the course of her work Dr Drown made the discovery that it was possible not only to diagnose the disease of a patient from a distance, but also to treat that patient from a distance using a sample of blood from the individual concerned.

During the 1940's a great deal of research was initiated at the Delawarr Laboratories in England. Once again instruments and techniques were refined and improved and much research was undertaken in the field of radionic photography. Today Radionics continues to keep pace with recent scientific developments and the modern practitioner, in keeping with the scientific axiom that 'All is Energy', looks upon his patients not only in physical terms but as a series of interpenetrating energy fields. He finds concepts in the ancient philosophies which deal with man as a multi-concentric energy system, concepts which tie in with modern discoveries, and it may thus be said that Radionics is a field of activity where physics and para-physics, science and religion, meet and merge.

SOME FUNDAMENTAL CONCEPTS OF RADIONICS

Basic to radionic theory and practice is the concept that man and all life-forms share a common ground in that they are submerged in the electro-magnetic energy field of the earth; and further, that each life-form has its own electromagnetic field which, if sufficiently distorted, will ultimately result in disease of the organism.

Accepting that 'All is Energy', Radionics sees organs, diseases and remedies as having their own particular frequency or vibration. These factors can be expressed in numerical values and are known in Radionics as 'Rates'; hence the calibrated dials of the radionic instruments upon which the frequencies or 'Rates' can be placed for diagnostic or treatment purposes.

One final and important concept in Radionics is that the electro-magnetic or Life-field of the earth, with its subtler variety of frequencies which lie beyond the electro-magnetic spectrum, provides the link between patient and practitioner during analysis and treatment. It is an ancient axiom that 'Energy follows Thought' and that thought is transmitted through the energy field of the earth; in this way the practitioner can attune himself to the patient.

THE TECHNIQUE OF RADIONICS

The radionic practitioner in making his analysis utilizes the principles of dowsing by applying his faculties of extra-sensory perception (ESP) to the problem of detecting disease in much the same way that the dowser detects the location of water, oil or mineral deposits. The particular form of ESP used in Radionics is often referred to as the radiesthetic faculty through which the practitioner, by means of a series of mentally posed questions, obtains information relative to the health of his patient to which the conscious, thinking mind has no direct access.

In the early days of Radionics it was usually necessary for the patient to be present when an analysis was made and the treatment given. Today this is no longer the case as it has been found that a blood spot or a snippet of hair will serve to establish the necessary link with the patient through the medium of the earth's energy field.

Thus, the standard practice when a Radionic practitioner is consulted is for the patient to send the practitioner a blood spot or hair sample accompanied by a case history and a full description of symptoms. If convenient, however, some practitioners like to see the patient in person for an initial consultation. In order to make an analysis the practitioner places the patient's sample on his radionic instrument, then attunes his mind to the patient and adjusts his instrument in a way which is analogous to the adjustment, or tuning, of a radio to receive a distant transmission. This having been done the practitioner, aided by his knowledge of anatomy, physiology and the nature of the human force field, proceeds to pose a series of questions in a methodical and predetermined order relative to the nature of the patient's illness and the causative factors involved.

A radionic analysis is not a medical diagnosis, but a means of identifying and assessing the underlying causes which give rise to pathological states and their symptoms. These may or may not coincide with current medical opinion, but this is to be expected when the practitioner's approach is along para-physical lines and he is

concerned with causative factors which may not be clinically identifiable or measurable.

RADIONIC TREATMENT

When the radionic analysis is complete and the practitioner has
accurately ascertained the major causative factors of the patient's illness, he determines what form of treatment is required by the patient
to remove those factors. As all pathological states and their causes
have their own particular frequency or vibration, he selects those
'Rates' which will offset the imbalance or disease in the patient's
system. These 'Rates' are projected or transmitted by the practitioner to the patient by means of a radionic treatment instrument,
once again using the blood spot or hair sample as a link. Some practitioners use, as an adjunct to the healing influence of the 'Rate',
homoeopathic, Bach (flower) or other similar remedies. These are
placed on the instrument in proximity to the patient's sample.

It may be difficult to accept that such treatment can be effective at
a distance. However, the weight of clinical evidence shows that it is
very effective in a significant number of cases. 'Action at a distance',
as this phenomenon is called, is not new to science, today a great deal
of research is being carried out by scientific institutions in this field
and they are finding that both humans and plants respond to projected thought patterns and that this phenomenon occurs no matter
how great is the distance between the subjects under investigation.
Their findings now bear out the rationale of Radionics.

Additionally or alternatively, the radionic practitioner may re-
commend other forms of treatment such as changes in the patient's
diet, osteopathic or chiropractic manipulation, homoeopathic or
herbal remedies; or, if the nature of the case warrants medical attention, he will refer the patient to his Doctor, thus in all instances
making sure that the patient receives that form of treatment which
will restore harmony to his being.

One of the advantages of a radionic analysis is that it is often possible to discover from it potentially serious conditions at an early
stage and, by appropriate treatment, to prevent them developing to
the point at which they become clinically identifiable. Moreover, as
radionic treatment takes place on a non-physical level it cannot harm
any living tissue or produce any unnatural side effects.

RADIONICS - AN ENTELECHTIC APPROACH TO HEALING

Entelechy is defined in the medical dictionary as 'Completion; full

development or realization; the complete expression of some function. A vital principle operating in living creatures as a directive
spirit'. Radionics, by its very nature, is an entelechtic or holistic approach to healing; it is above all concerned with the total man, with
his mind, his emotions and with the subtle force fields that govern the
functioning and well-being of his visible organic systems. Orthodox
science has devoted its attention almost exclusively to the many vari-
eties of disease and in the process it seems to have lost sight of the individual. Conversely, Radionics is concerned with the healing of the
whole man, with the health pattern or entelechy of the individual.
This health pattern is a singular, unitary force within the structures
of man that ensures adequate and optimum functioning of the
systems of his body. The purpose of radionic therapy is to help the individual to re-establish his optimum pattern of health.

INTRODUCTION

My first book *Radionics and The Subtle Anatomy of Man* was written primarily for radionic practitioners, because I felt there was a need to call attention to those aspects of man which lay beyond the physical mechanism. It was clear that the teachings of the Ancient Wisdom had a very direct and practical application to the practice of radionics, and would enhance its value as a diagnostic and therapeutic technique.

Response to the book from radionic practitioners has been very satisfying. Many have incorporated the techniques it outlines in their day to day practice to good effect, and the School of Radionics now includes the subject of the subtle anatomy of man and the basic principles of Centre Therapy in its training programme.

Judging by the number of letters and even phone calls that have come from countries as far away as America, Australia, New Zealand, Malaysia and South Africa, this book struck a responsive chord in other fields. Doctors of medicine, osteopaths, masseurs, physiotherapists, healers and many lay people have contacted me, some seeking further knowledge along these lines, others wanting to share their knowledge, ideas and experiences, and some wanting to help with matters of health.

The central theme of response to 'Radionics and The Subtle Anatomy of Man' has been quite singular. People have said that it takes a complicated subject like the subtle bodies of man, and presents it in a simple yet practical and informative manner. Many practitioners, especially those who have physical contact with their patients, like masseurs, physiotherapists, osteopaths and chiropractors, have through reading the book come to a realization that the subtle bodies of man are an immediate reality, and that they have been working with these subtle aspects, often unconsciously, in their practices. The concepts contained in the book have in some measure broadened their whole idea of health and healing within the framework of their own particular discipline. This has happened, I believe, because a knowledge of such matters is basic to any healing art, be it radionics, homoeopathy, chiropractic or any other method.

In this book which should be considered a companion volume to my first, the central theme is going to be radionics and radionic practice in relationship to the force field in which we live and move and have our being, thus it will once again have appeal to practitioners in other disciplines and to students of the Wisdom Teachings. I feel most strongly that in an understanding of broad basic principles, especially those connected with the Life-field we live in, there lies a common bond of harmony to be shared by all of the healing arts.

Against the backdrop of the energy field we live in I am going to touch upon a theory which attempts to explain how the radionic practitioner links with his patient over distances of thousands of miles in order to diagnose and treat. This theory brings metaphysical considerations forward and relates them directly to organic and cellular analogs.

Even more remarkable is the fact that radionic cameras, linked to a blood spot can photograph the internal organs of the donor of that sample, over any distance. Or is it remarkable? Dr Ruth Drown didn't seem to think so and she was the first in the world to discover this technique. I will explore some of the facets of this rather mind stretching subject in the hope that perhaps it will stimulate some to investigate this phenomena, and increase in others the recognition that we all share a common field of energy, a knowledge of which is of use to anyone who serves in the healing arts.

Ruth Drown not only pioneered radionic photography, but she also had the idea that if you could 'pull' photographs out of the ethers, why not homoeopathic remedies. Today, as we shall see, this has been developed into a fine art and radionic potency simulation is here to stay, and I might add used by a growing number of medical doctors, osteopaths and radionic practitioners throughout the world.

Like *Radionics and The Subtle Anatomy of Man* this volume will cover other practical aspects dealing with radionic diagnostic and therapeutic techniques for the practitioner. But like its companion, is just an introduction to a vast subject. It is written with one thought in mind, and that is to stimulate the reader to look further, to consider without prejudging, ideas and concepts that may on first sight seem way out, but on second thoughts and with a bit of study begin to make sense and open up whole new vistas, whole new areas of ideas and heretofore unconsidered levels of consciousness.

Radionics of course is not a scientific subject in the accepted sense of the word, but this in no way invalidates its profound value to those who practice it, nor to those who receive the benefits of treatment. People are fast becoming disenchanted with the more orthodox methods of healing, not because they are without value, but because they tend to strip man of his dignity, and to annihilate any feelings he may have about being a part of the universal scheme of things. Carl Jung probably summed this up better than anyone when he said: 'People have become weary of scientific specialization and rationalistic intellectualism. They want to hear truths which do not make them narrower but broader, which do not obscure but enlighten, which do not run off them like water, but pierce them to the marrow.'

There are of course a growing number of scientists and doctors who are interested in radionics; among them Professor William Tiller of Stanford University in California, who has made a study of the subject and written papers on it. No doubt many others will follow and one day science will take time to consider radionics seriously and recognise it as a field worthy of proper investigation and study.

Radionics like any body of knowledge may be likened to a crystal, each facet representing a particular aspect. Where these facets relate to another body of knowledge an interface occurs and across an interface a common bond of harmony can be expressed, and energy exchanges in terms of information can be exchanged and separative attitudes dispelled. Radionics has many interfaces with a variety of other bodies of knowledge, particularly medicine, physics, healing and the study of human thought in action. Radionics is also unique in that it has the potential to link spiritual concepts with orthodox ones, especially in the field of healing, an area where they are desperately needed.

Today the interest in radionics grows apace. The demand for any literature pertaining to the subject has never been so great because people are recognizing the intrinsic value of radionics, both from a philosophical point of view and as a healing art that seeks out the causative factors in disease. Many are finding that chronic problems of health which have plagued them for years and resisted all efforts to cure, give way and are eliminated in a way that is subtle and without side effects. They find themselves enjoying good health again, which speaks for the efficacy of this form of treatment at a distance. There may be no scientific statistics to show that radionics works, but there are a great many people who feel better for it.

Chapter One

AN ESOTERIC ETHER-FIELD CONSTRUCT

'The acceptance of the reality of an etheric body that interpenetrates the material state is the sine qua non of every radionic operator. This etheric body appears to function in a sea of vital etheric energy that is actually fundamental to the material forces of magnetism and electricity.'
Radionic Newsletter (Spring 1968)
George de la Warr

For a real understanding of radionics it is essential to grasp the concept that we live in a vast energy field, and that in this field, actions and inter-actions continually occur that relate both to our well-being and to the processes of our inner development. Every action, every thought one has reverberates through this energy field and according to its nature, either retards or enhances the evolutionary progress of the individual and ultimately the Being he lives within.

Obviously we can make better use of the energy field we live in if we have some basic knowledge of its structure and function. This is particularly true if one practices radionic therapy, because in radionics we are utilizing this field day in and day out for healing purposes. Knowledge, as Meister Eckhart once pointed out, is power, and clearly knowledge of the ether-fields gives to the radionic practitioner the power to diagnose and treat in a more esoteric and subtle manner.

What follows is brief and to the point. It is simply an outline of the ether-fields in which man lives and has his being, in accordance with the teachings of the ancient wisdom. As radionic practitioners we can use this outline as a working hypothesis for the theories and practice of radionics. This outline, as I have already pointed out is very basic, and it is up to the individual once he has an understanding of it to add details from other sources. In this way a growing knowledge of the ether-fields will lead to a growing understanding and ultimately a greater expertise in identifying and manipulating the healing energies present in it. This of course not only applies to radionic practitioners

1

but to those who do any healing work.

I think it worth mentioning that charts similar to this are being used in scientific circles. Dr Elmer Green, Director of the Psychophysiological Laboratory of the Menninger Foundation, and Director of the Psychosynthesis Institute used a similar chart to illustrate his talk, 'How to make use of the Mind-Field Theory' this can be seen in the Transcript of The Dimensions of Healing, held at Stanford University in California, September 1972. On the same symposium Professor William Tiller speaks of using a similar model in his lecture, 'Consciousness, Radiation and the developing Sensory System'. Professor Tiller is head of the Material Sciences Department at Stanford University and a consultant to industry and the American government in metallurgy and solid state physics. He is also an international authority on the science of crystalization. Both Professor Tiller and Dr Green have drawn material from the writings of Alice Bailey; the former even goes on to discuss the chakras and refers to them as major energy transducers. In this manner the esoteric teachings are being utilized and will gradually find acceptance at these levels.

As the chart has details of the subtle anatomy of man, perhaps it would be as well to summarize them briefly.

Man as a reflection of the Macrocosm is formed of the trinity of Spirit, Soul and Body. The Spirit of man frequently referred to as the Monad is also threefold in nature, consisting of a unified triad of Will, Love, Wisdom and Active Intelligence: in other words we have the Trinity of Father, Son and Holy Ghost to use Christian terminology. Or we may have this triad Purpose, Love and Intelligence or, more abstractly, Positive Energy, Balanced Energy and Negative Energy.

The monad is the immortal part of man that reincarnates, it is the germinal Spirit containing the.potentialities of Divinity. It has nothing whatsoever to do with the Spiritualist term spirit, which can mean anything from a discarnate entity to a vague area out of which messages emanate. Spirit can be symbolized by a Triangle (or the equal armed cross).

In order to incarnate the Monad or Spiritual man appropriates six stable force centres: around these the subtle bodies are built. These force centres are known as permanent atoms, of which there are five, plus what is known as a mental unit. Permanent atoms are those atoms which have come under the attractive power of the second aspect of the Monad, the Son or Christ aspect.

The ordinary atoms of our bodies are vitalized by the third or Mother aspect. These permanent atoms are the storehouses of

THE SUBTLE BODIES OF MAN IN THE ETHER FIELDS

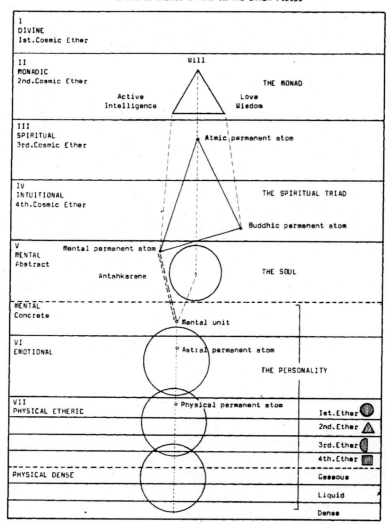

karma, often spoken of as the 'Arbiters of Fate.' They are, if you like, data memory banks which determine the nature and quality of our bodies.

Now the Will aspect of the Monad links with what is known as the Atmic Permanent atom. The Wisdom aspect links with the Buddhic Permanent atom and the third aspect of Intelligence or Mind links with what is called the Manasic Permanent atom. So the Monad expresses its first step towards incarnation through a triangle energy.

The reaction of each of these three points of the triangle produces activity on what is called the higher mental plane, and this activity produces a force centre or lotus which we call the soul. The soul consists of twelve petals surrounding a latent point of fire.

This can be symbolized by a circle divided into twelve sections. These are the twelve signs of the zodiac, the twelve gates and twelve foundation stones to the City of Jerusalem, the twelve disciples at the Last Supper in the Upper Chamber. On the physical level we have the twelve cranial nerves. One of them, as I have mentioned, is the Vagus which links the head and heart, the passage way for the breath of the Holy Spirit.

As one penetrates the meaning of the subtle anatomy of man, one cannot help but take a different view of pathology; for example, Trigeminal neuralgia, or as it is commonly called, 'tic doloreux', is then recognized not merely as an inflammatory state of one of the cranial nerves, but a deep malaise existing between the soul and its vehicles of expression in the three worlds. The soul then is the vehicle of manifestation for the Spirit and through it the Spirit ultimately gains control of the matter of the levels below the soul.

These levels or 'three worlds' as they are called in the Indian teachings are the mental, the emotional or astral level and the physical which also includes the etheric levels. The soul, in order to penetrate deeper into matter, sounds its note, activating the permanent atoms of the low-self, and in deep meditation produces a thoughtform which eventually precipitates upon the physical plane as a human being. Withdrawal of the soul's attention from this work of thoughtform building results in a still birth.

A viable thought-form consists of a mental body, an astral or emotional body and an etheric body which is the archetype for the physical form. The low-self then is also a triad of forms, but the etheric and physical may be considered as separate bodies and this then gives us the City which lies foursquare, and is in fact represented by a square. Thus we have the New Jerusalem of The Book of Revelation where the Square of the low-self and the Circle of the Soul are reconciled by the Equal Armed Cross of the Spirit.

We are all familiar I am sure with the phrase, 'don't be a square,' which was part of the hip talk of the fifties and early sixties. Curiously enough such jargon is an unconscious expression of an esoteric truth. One of course should not be a square, or in other words a person wholly concerned with the low-self. You may recall that the late sixties brought us Flower Power, wherein the ideal was love and peace, both attributes of the soul or 'Ultimate Flower', as Migual Serrano calls it in his book of that title.

Flower Power was quickly undermined by drugs made available through the agencies of the forces of Ahriman ... Many young people were quickly diverted back into the world of astral and psychedelic phenomena, back into the realm of the Square, a form through which spiritual forces do not readily flow, but illusory factors abound.

The Revelations of St John are an excellent treatise on the subtle anatomy of man, and they pay particular attention to the chakras and the flow of spiritual forces through these gateways. When John wrote:

'And I saw in the right hand of him that sat on the throne a book written within and on the back, sealed with seven seals'

he was talking of the seven major chakras which govern man and his actions. There follows details of the inter-actions of these centres as man unfolds his spiritual nature: there is much to be learned from his vision on Patmos.

It is not my intention to go into any details relevant to the action of one chakra upon another and the alterations to the states of consciousness that occur during such action. I have simply tried to give but the briefest of outlines of the subtle anatomy of man in order to show you that it is not something vague, but a definite form constructed from various grades of matter, and that in every aspect of its nature and form it reveals the Nature of the Divine man in which we live and move and have our being.

Those who have heeded the Delphic injunction, 'Know Thyself', and have conscientiously sought to map the inner levels of their being will be somewhat familiar with what I have outlined. Now why should the esoteric constitution of man and the ether fields concern us?

Well, for a start, I would tentatively put forward the suggestion that any healer, physician or radionic practitioner who is actively and consciously seeking to work along New Age lines, should have an extensive and intimate knowledge of the subtle anatomy of man, and an ever growing cognizance of the forces that go into its makeup, and of those energies which flow through it as man seeks to express himself. Similarly, he should be able to determine the imbalances in energy flow relative to the pathology manifested in his patient.

In other words, he will be seeking out the cause of disease rather than treating the pathological state itself. Above all he will be fully aware of what type of energy he needs to select for purposes of treatment.

When we attend a medical doctor for help we expect that he has undergone a rigorous training and discipline to learn his art, and that he has a detailed knowledge of human anatomy and physiology, and of the diseases that plague the human form. Similarly, we expect him to know the medicines or remedies that are needed to help us rid our bodies of disease.

I put to you that in the not-too-distant future the same will be demanded of the healer. He will have to undergo rigorous training involving a detailed knowledge of the esoteric constitution of man, and he will have to become aware of the quality of the energies he wields as he seeks to help his patients. Most certainly he will have to function consciously as a soul, taking full responsibility for what he does.

It will no longer suffice that his practice be based solely on a desire to help others; it will have to be based on direct perception and knowledge of the inner levels of life. The day will pass when healers have little or no knowledge of the subtle bodies of man and next to no knowledge of the type and intensity of the energies they are wielding and directing through their patients. Responsibility will replace the attitude that 'something up there' switches off the power for them when the healing is done.

Now let us get back to the chart. These seven planes of energy represent the physical plane of the Solar Being in which we live and move and have our being. They are in effect His etheric and physical bodies. The chart clearly shows these levels and it should be realized that they do not in fact appear one above the other as illustrated but as a series of interpenetrating energy fields.

The four ethers are referred to in the writings of Rudolf Steiner in the following manner. The first ether is called the warmth ether and its formative force produces the spherical shapes we see in Nature. It is the ether of electricity.

The second ether is called the light-ether and its formative action gives rise to triangular shapes. It is as the name suggests the ether of light.

The third ether is called the chemical-ether and out of its activity there arises half-moon forms. This is the ether of sound and of numbers.

The fourth ether is known as the life-ether and this gives rise to square and elongated rectangular forms. This is the ether of colour.

Plane I	Divine.	First cosmic ether.
Plane II	Monadic.	Second cosmic ether. The level where the Spirit of man has its being.
Plane III	Spiritual.	Third cosmic ether.
Plane IV	Intuitional.	Fourth cosmic ether.
Plane V	Mental.	Cosmic gaseous plane. This is divided into two aspects. First the abstract mental level upon which the soul of man appears. Secondly the lower concrete mind, this is the thinking apparatus of man and forms the first vehicle of the lower-self or personality. The mental body is made of cosmic gaseous matter.
Plane VI	Astral.	Cosmic liquid plane. Here forms the astral or emotional body of man made up of cosmic liquid matter gathered around the astral permanent atom.
Plane VII	Physical-etheric.	The physical etheric level is made up of four ethers which form the etheric body of man and three other levels of matter which are gaseous, liquid and dense form the physical body. Thus man the microcosm is physically a reflection of the macrocosm.

Although science does not recognize these ethers, they are in effect a part of the electro-magnetic field that does have orthodox recognition. George de la Warr in the course of his researches came to the conclusion that the pre-physical state of etheric energy could be considered as complementary to electromagnetic energy. The esoteric teachings have always stated that ALL life is of an electromagnetic nature and it helps us in our understanding of these force fields if we can get over the habit of separating out in our minds the esoteric and scientific viewpoints. Try viewing them as a whole.

Each one of these elements, electro-magnetic force, light, sound, numbers and colour are of concern to the radionic practitioner, for they are the factors he uses in conjunction with the power of directed thought and visualization to project healing frequencies through these ether-bands to the patient.

In a *Treatise on White Magic* by Alice Bailey, three reasons for gaining an understanding of the etheric body are pointed out to the student of the esoteric teachings. They are listed here because they apply equally to radionic practitioners, for they contain a basis for a deeper understanding of the theory and practice of radionics.

1   The etheric body is the next aspect of the world substance to be studied by scientists and investigators. This time will be hastened if thinking men and women can formulate intelligent ideas anent this interesting subject. We can aid in the revelation of truth by our clear thinking and from the standpoint of the present pronouncements about the ether, scientists will eventually arrive at an understanding of etheric forms or bodies.

2   The etheric body is composed of force currents, and in it are vital centres linked by lines of force with each other and with the nervous system of the physical man. Through these lines of force, it is connected also with the etheric body of the environing system. Note that in this lies the basis for a belief in immortality, for the law of brotherhood or unity and for astrological truth.

3   The need of realizing that the etheric body is vitalized and controlled by thought and can (through thought) be brought into full functioning activity.

If one can grasp the full import of the contents of these three statements, realizing their inner essence that in fact there is no separation between any object on the physical – etheric plane, that you and I and everybody and everything is inter-connected, and that this interconnectedness can be utilized, through the use of clearly formulated thought patterns and visualization to heal at a distance, your capacity to work on these levels will be greatly enhanced.

In her book called 'Telepathy and the Etheric Vehicle' Alice Bailey writes:

'The force of mind. This is the illuminating energy which "Lights the way" of an idea or form to be transmitted and received. Forget not that light is a subtle substance. Upon a beam of light can the energy of the mind materialize.'

We shall see that this concept lies at the heart of the transmission of healing energies by radionic means, and Ruth Drown even goes so far as to write of this 'beam of light' being used in radionic photography. There can be no doubt that an understanding of the ether fields is of vital importance to any practitioner of radionics if he or she is to progress more deeply into the arcana of this healing art.

Chapter Two

THE CONNECTIVE TISSUE OF SPACE

'. . . it must be carefully borne in mind that the etheric body of every form in nature is an integral part of the substantial form of God Himself – not the dense physical form, but what the esotericists regard as the form-making substance.'

Telepathy and the Etheric Vehicle
AAB

In September 1962 an American journal called *Main Currents in Modern Thought* waived its usual presentation procedure in order to concentrate upon a topic which its editors felt to be one of the most important and critical of all philosophical and educational problems of our time, namely the reality of the non-material cosmos and its relationship to the sensed world of everyday experience. In other words, they dealt in depth with the electro-dynamic theory of life; with the electro-magnetic fields of energy in which all life moves and has its being.

The average individual tends to equate space with the gaps that exist between physical objects, as something that is empty. The ancient seers on the other hand defined space as a formative matrix, as an energy field which gives birth to matter. They saw it as the very essence of Nature, without shape and timeless, underlying all forms, all qualities and all events.

The concept of subtle force fields underlying all physical forms is of very ancient origin. The Vedas of India, thousands of years ago posed the question: 'What is the origin of this world?' and answered: 'Ether . . . for all these beings take their rise from the ether only, and return into the ether. Ether is greater than these, ether is their rest.'

Plato spoke of an archetypal essence which he felt contained the predetermining images of the world we see about us. Similarly the alchemists spoke of the Nous and Paracelsus of the Archeus when referring to the light or energy that underlies the world of shadow or form in which we live. Their emphasis has always been upon the underlying essence, upon the vast force fields that give rise to matter.

More recently, in 1675, Newton presented his 'Second Paper on Light and Colours' to the Royal Society in which he spoke of an electro-magnetic like 'subtle ... vibrating ... electric and elastic medium' as the inorganic basis of life. In 1704 Mead spoke of atmospheric tides, which, he propounded, acted as an 'external assistance to the inward causes prevailing in animal bodies . . .' and he equated the 'nervous fluid', as it was called, with electricity. Two men, Nollet and Freke, published related theories in 1747 and 1752. Next was Mesmer, who helped himself to Mead's notion of atmospheric tides and added to it Newton's 'vibrating . . . electric and elastic' spirit.

At first Mesmer called it 'animal gravitation' but in 1775 he changed it to the more familiar 'animal magnetism'. This medium filling celestial space, was believed capable of acting on the nervous systems of animal forms directly, depending on the individual tidal resonances in human bodies. Such harmonics were supposedly attuned to specific astronomic configurations.

In 1783 Bertholon published his experiments providing evidence for the influence of atmospheric electricity on vegetation. In 1883 a man named Stewart reformulated Mead's theory positing the electric conductivity of the earth's upper atmosphere.

1913 saw Dr Albert Abrams, the father of modern radionics, give his first public demonstration of recognizing and measuring the human energy field in health and disease. He spoke of electropathology and also used the word electronics long before it became the familiar word it is today. Through his instruments he used weak, pulsating electro-magnetic currents to restore health to diseased bodies.

All this leads us to 1935 when Northrupp and Burr updated Mead's theory and showed that what held good for inorganic matter should hold true in the biological domain. In other words they posited that organic forms are related to underlying electro-magnetic force fields. So, from ancient times, man has come full circle and from the depths of a materialistically oriented science he is now forced to face the intangible, but with one great difference: today he has electronic instruments so sensitive that they can measure with complete accuracy the electro-magnetic or Life-fields as they are called, and this has far reaching implications in all fields of human endeavour, especially those of healing and philosophy.

Modern field physics is a complicated and technical subject for the specialist, however I am of the opinion that radionic practitioners should have, for a variety of reasons, a basic knowledge of the electro-dynamic theory of life. Firstly, in radionics, we are dealing with force fields of one kind or another, with action at a distance which presupposes a force field through which that action takes place. The radionic practitioner generally accepts that in one way or another he utilizes the electro-magnetic field of the earth when diagnosing and treating patients at a distance, but there is no doubt in his mind that he also uses other fields, fields that are far more subtle in nature and beyond identification and measurement in the scientifically accepted sense. In this way his thinking tends to align itself with both the concepts of the Ancient Wisdom and with the findings of science.

For the present this places the radionic practitioner in a comfortable position. He has a broad philosophical horizon, and, on the other hand he is not in a bind to have to prove himself as the scientist does. Thus he can use his abilities in the satisfying pursuit of getting people well, often people that modern science with all of its wonder drugs and technology has failed to heal.

The work of Dr Saxton Burr is no doubt one of the most significant steps forward that science has made in which the emphasis has shifted from the physical to the subtle, and the intangible is being made tangible through controlled and repeated scientific experimentation.

For the moment, let us look a little more closely at the electro-dynamic theory of life. This material is drawn in the main from Dr Burr's recent book *Blueprint for Immortality*, a book incidentally, that is written with such direct simplicity that any layman can grasp and benefit from its content. To begin with I would like to quote from Dr Burr's Foreword to his book, it says:

'The Universe in which we find ourselves and from which we cannot be separated is a place of Law and Order. It is not an accident, nor chaos. It is organised and maintained by an electro-dynamic Field capable of determining the position and movement of all charged particles. For nearly half a century the logical consequences of this theory have been subjected to rigorously controlled experimental conditions and met with no contradictions.'

It is no surprise that Dr Burr's first chapter is in a philosophical vein. He speaks of the troubled times we live in where crime, war and lawlessness are in ceaseless eruption and more and more people are forced to ask themselves whether life has any sense or purpose. Many, he says, are tempted to believe that man is an accident, left to grapple with his lonely fate on this insignificant planet in a harsh and lawless Universe. The materialistic and scientific age has made it hard to sustain his religious beliefs and he demands some scientific proof of his relationship with life and the Universe.

Dr Burr felt that this demand had been met and that science can show man that he has his place in the Universe and that his form is ordered and controlled by electro-dynamic fields. He goes on to say that organization and direction, the direct opposite of chance, imply purpose. So the fields of life offer purely electronic, instrumental evidence that man is no accident. On the contrary he is an integral part of the Cosmos, embedded in its all-powerful fields, subject to its inflexible laws and participant in the destiny and purpose of the Universe.

Electro-dynamic fields are invisible and intangible but their action, says Dr Burr, can be visualized in a rough way by placing a magnet under a card and sprinkling iron filings over it. The filings arrange themselves in the patterns of the lines of force of the magnet's field. If the filings are thrown away and fresh ones scattered on the card, the new filings will assume the same pattern as the old. Something similar, though very much more complicated, happens in the human body. Its molecules and cells are constantly being broken down and rebuilt with fresh material from the food we eat and no doubt from the other various energies we absorb. Due to the controlling Life-field the new molecules and cells rebuild as before and arrange themselves in the same pattern. Thus a physical form retains its familiar and recognizable shape.

Modern research has shown that the material of our bodies is renewed very frequently. For example, all the protein in the body is 'turned over' every six months and in some organs such as the liver, the protein is renewed more frequently. If we meet someone we have not seen for six months there is not one molecule in his face which was there when we last saw him. But thanks to the controlling L-field the new molecules have moved into the same pattern which is familiar to us and we recognize him.

Dr Burr likens the Life-field to a jelly-mould which will produce a predictable shape. Similarly the L-field can be measured, and in its initial stage for example, a frog's egg when examined with electronic apparatus will show the future location of the frog's nervous system. A scientific theory has been put forward that the human nervous system forms as a result of dynamic forces imposed on cell groups by the total field pattern. Moreover, with the vertical evolution of nervous organization, field correlates of state changes provide evidence for the 'dynamo' function of the basal ganglia and associated nuclei; an ancient and intermediary storage depot for supplying energy that must reach a certain level before neocortical activity eventuates. This, beyond a doubt, ties in with the theory of the chakras, which, as vortices of energy, give birth to the ganglia and the nerve plexuses of the body.

The apparatus used to measure L-fields is a vacuum tube volt-meter which is sensitive enough to pick up the changes occurring in the electro-dynamic field. In humans the L-field can be measured by placing an electrode on the forehead and another on the chest or hand, and then finding the voltage differential between these two points. Dr Abrams in his radionic research and practice did exactly the same thing with much cruder instruments. One wonders what great strides would have been made in diagnosis and healing if the genius of Abrams were wedded to modern electronics. Even in his day he designed and built an instrument that automatically gave off a different note or sound for each of the three major diseases as various blood spots were introduced into it. His problem was the material at hand, for the valves blew so constantly and quickly that it made the instrument impracticable and it had to be abandoned. However, it indicated the possibilities.

The ancient teachers claimed that all life shares one vast, common ground, the lowest manifestation of which they referred to as the etheric levels. When an individual grasps the full import of this fact in his consciousness, his attitude to other life-forms alters. He recognizes, if you like, that he is in them and they are in him. What hurts or helps him has repercussions on other life-forms in and beyond time and space which are not immediately evident on the apparent separativeness of the physical level.

The advent of Dr Burr's work heralded the first scientific step into the subtle force fields of life. Although this was science in action the immediate implication was a philosophical one, and this, as we have seen, is fully expressed in his opening chapter. The discovery of Life-fields has, of course, had an effect upon medicine both in the physical and psychological areas of research and practice. Health, it has been found, is inextricably linked to field states. The state of your Life-field and your vitality has a direct relationship to the state of the earth's electro-magnetic field and the fluctuations that occur in that field due to influences flowing in from space. This is rather nicely illustrated by the following extract from *Studies of Man in the Life Field* by Dr L. Ravitz. He writes:

'One hot, humid June afternoon near new moon, two waitresses forget to serve their customers. Office help is drowsy and works perfunctorily. Elderly persons complain of profound lassitude. There is a large influx of new admissions on all hospital services with greatly increased birth and death rates – the latter pronounced during afternoon hours – and patients begin to have markedly increased somatic symptoms. Almost half the psychiatric patients require increased supervision, and three are now suicidal.

Certain abstinent alcoholics start to drink again, and crimes are rampant.

Two weeks later, the waitresses snap irritably at customers. Most of the office staff feel unusually energetic, the rest equally irritable. Elderly persons feel a 'second wind'. Another influx of hospital admissions occurs, but medical and surgical patients seem to have less intense symptoms. A different group of psychiatric patients is 'going into orbit', but none have been actively suicidal. Complaints of insomnia are widespread, as are comments on unusually vivid dreams.'

Consider the direct correlation of the following passages drawn from the Agni Yoga series of books, which incidentally are a mine of information for those who would like to relate esoteric teachings to modern thought. The first passage is from *Brotherhood*.

'It is unthinkable not to sense the tension of the cosmic currents which absorb the psychic energy. There may be apparent a certain drowsiness, there may be absent-mindedness, as it were, there may be involuntary irritation – it is instructive to observe these signs that accompany the absorption of energy. People are inclined to attribute them to their own indisposition, but let us not forget the external causes.'

The second passage is drawn from the book *Aum*.

'A great number of painful sensations are caused by psycho-atmospheric tensions. We do not mean atmospheric pressures only, but actual psychic waves, which can not only create moods but can reflect upon the nerve centres. One cannot imagine to what extent the atmosphere is saturated by psychic energies; such emanations produce effects not only upon animal life but also upon plants. Therefore, it is impossible light-mindedly to attribute all these manifestations merely to crude physical conditions . . .'

These passages must have a familiar ring to many radionic practitioners for most have experienced the sudden and inexplicable increases in the number of phone calls from patients who do not feel right and are not altogether sure what is wrong with them, or suddenly they will get a whole series of patients phoning with a similar ailment that has just made its appearance. In radionics one has the chance to observe this phenomenon, and I am sure that it has a direct relationship to the interaction of the patient's Life-field with that of the planetary and systemic Life-field, clearly the fluctuations of geomagnetic tides flowing across this earth must be considered in radionics.

Medically, much work has been done in correlating the periods of electro-magnetic field strength intensification and subsequent influxes of hospital admissions to the psychiatric service. Patient's reactions to the surrounding and interpenetrating field state in which we live can be accurately predicted from a few hours up to six and twelve months ahead of time. In this manner they are able to be prepared for the future predictable actions and therefore requirements of their patients. Cyclic timing, for example, of hay fever and peptic ulcers can be similarly related to such polarity changes.

For example, individuals who have periodic peptic ulcer symptoms tend to show field patterns at the minus end of the polarity spectrum all the year round, with symptom exacerbations during those seasonal, fortnightly and diurnal periods when voltages dip into the highest-minus values. Since sudden fear or startle responses are typically associated with field excursions in the plus direction, it follows that persons suffering from high-minus symptoms would feel temporary relief if fear action were evoked. This has been noted experimentally and in real life situations. For example such an individual may come out of a car crash with a feeling of exhilaration as though he were on a 'high', and not at any time experience shock beyond the physical contusions that may have occurred.

Discovery of the field direction, be it plus or minus, as a crucial variable in ageing and somatic disturbances has important implications in the epidemiology of infectious diseases. In his studies of diphtheria in the 1920's and 1930's, Frost observed that infection per case ratio could vary greatly in a given area in time; he then suggested that infection remains relatively constant, and that epidemic ebb and flow probably represented the consequence of variations in the infection per case ratio. Recent monitoring of electro-magnetic fields shows that there is a link between field flow and strength and the movement and intensity of epidemics. Dr Burr predicted the day would come when the vacuum tube voltmeter would be in common use in every doctor's office and the patient's health or disease will be discussed in terms of energy potential.

Careful study of forecast disturbances in the earth's electro-magnetic field shows a frequent coincidence with observable phenomena. For example on the day of the Yellowstone Park earthquake in the USA, which began near midnight on August 17th, 1959, the forecast showed storm warning signals of high intensity. About noon on that day, twelve miles west of the Park at Lake Hegben, a favourite resting-place for migrating water fowl, there was a sudden and general exodus of the birds. It appears that they were aware of the disturbance in the earth's magnetic field eleven hours before the earthquake. The field disturbance of the same date caused a severe radio blackout of world-wide range. The cable system of New York's Consolidated Edison was affected so that service was cut for many hours. And on that day a missile launching of the NIKE ASP failed. It is a known fact that some dowsing operations, such as searching for water can at times be hampered if there are unusual disturbances in the electro-magnetic field of the earth.

There is a group in America known as Geomagnetics Research. They began a study around 1940 with the discovery of a predictive index, based on an astronomical frame of reference, for the advance timing of field disturbance periods coinciding with radio blackouts and solar storms. In 1962 this group found itself grappling with a demonstrated time parameter whose storm warning forecasts coincided not only with the geomagnetic storms, but with major earthquakes, volcanic eruptions, and since 1957 – with missile launching failures. The disastrous failure of the US Venus probe, on July 22nd, 1962, coincided with a high potential storm warning signal in the forecast.

If the launching of a rocket, an object which we normally consider to be an inert, rather mechanical piece of hardware, can be affected, it takes no imagination as to how these disturbances in the electro-magnetic field of the earth affect us.

This really brings us back to the concept of the ancient teachings, that all life is inextricably linked by a common ground, and that everything has an effect on that field of life and we can either pollute or harmonize this field through the thoughts and actions we express in it. As Dr Ravitz says in more scientific terms:

'Local field perturbations are conditioned by the state of the total field and the state of the total field is reciprocally conditioned by its local perturbations.'

In an article entitled 'The Wings of Hermes' Muriel Hasbrouck writes:

'All living creatures, including men, seem to respond organically and unconsciously to a reality which man may once have consciously known, but then forgotten. For it is apparent that so long ago as 3,200 years B.C., men were aware of the reality of the cosmic rhythms and of their possible relationship to the laws that governed life on earth. At that time the Sumerian priesthood inductively and empiracally plotted the paths of five visible planets "which moved in an established course, according to established laws, along the ways followed by the sun and moon among the fixed stars". . . . .'

It took the 19th century physicalism finally to diminish man to just another aggregate of material constituents and mechanical forces. So prevailing was this mood that Jung wrote, a few years before his death,

'The helpful view that man is a microcosm, a reflection of the great cosmos in miniature, has long since dropped away from him.'

Jung, through his work, demonstrated the profound healing influence inherent in the concept that man is a part of the Universe. He roused the image-making faculty in his patients and had them visualize themselves as linked with the macrocosm. Such a process can create a sense of inner and outer security, for the individual then finds himself no longer alone and separate, but an integral part of a continuous and unified reality. Dr Burr has shown that such a concept is a demonstrable fact; of course man yearns for more subtle expressions of unity and no doubt these will in time be expressed and capable of demonstration.

Suggestion, like imagination, has a marked effect upon the human electromagnetic field. Dr Abrams spoke of the tissues of the body as condensers which are reservoirs of surplus energy. They can be tapped by suggestion, an essential component of which is encouragement. Heretofore, he says, our knowledge was incapable of explaining the influence of the mind on the body. Let us express numerically and therefore without equivocation how much energy may be supplied by hope. He goes on:

> 'A depressed patient comes to my office and I find that the energy output from his left finger tips and psychomotor region is only 1/25 of an Ohm. He is assured of complete recovery and when this suggestion was accepted the energy output from his finger tips was 1 Ohm (an increase of 25 times) and from the left psychomotor region 15/25 of an Ohm.'

Belief and enthusiasm on the part of the healer or doctor does much to enhance the treatment he gives; such an attitude generates a powerful supply of energy which seems in some way to be transmitted to the patient. This is true in the practice of any healing art, even in medicine. There is an interesting example of this given in one of the talks on meditation and cancer therapy by Dr Carl Simonton, which demonstrates this point. A doctor who had devised a drug treatment for some particular ailment got excellent results with it. He then experimented and gave the patient a placebo, the patient became worse just as the doctor expected. He then ordered more of the drug, administered it, the patient got better again, but the drug company had in fact given the doctor another lot of placebos so it would appear that his belief in what he was giving had overridden the fact that there was no medicine in the tablets. Similar examples can be given in other healing fields which demonstrate that there is virtually no substitute for belief in what one is doing, and such belief can only be based on a real inner knowledge of the energy fields we live in when one works in the field of radionics.

If, as the experiments of Dr Burr have shown, we are being influenced by forces streaming in from space, it is reasonable to assume that there is some basis for astrology. In 1916 Abrams commented on this in the appendix of his book *New Concepts in Diagnosis and Treatment* when he wrote:

'Astrology began its decay at the renaissance but its revival can be forecast in terms of physical science. The attraction of man by the sun, the mechanical energy imparted to him by the sun and rotation of the earth, atmospheric pressure, variations in temperature, rain and winds, tremors of the earth and the electric potential at billions of volts all influence the microcosm by the macrocosm . . . the world machine.'

It would seem that Abrams made a very astute observation back in 1916, for today there can be little doubt that the work being done in astronomy and the studies and experiments of the electro-magnetic fields of life are bearing out what he predicted and further, they will no doubt one day bear out the ancient truths that man has faced away from during his explorations of the material worlds.

Relative to this I would like to quote the closing paragraph from the 1962 issue of *Main Currents* previously mentioned. It goes:

'. . . The main thing is that the research which takes us towards an understanding of life is uniquely important. In a time when all forms of life are under threat of extinction, and when the climate of thought is characterized by complexity and confusion, we have progressed a long way from the Pentagram of Pythagoras, the symbol of life, or the prana of Indian theory. It is time to reverse direction and face toward life, rather than death.'

Clearly today there is a powerful movement towards the recognition that man is a part of the Universe and that he has a role to play, a role of profound creative responsibility.

Now how does radionics fit into the present situation? If we go back to the early part of this century and look at the work of Abrams we find that he was talking about human beings and pathology in terms of electromagnetic energy fields, and he treated patients on this basis, by connecting them with an instrument which employed a weak electro-magnetic current. In terms of understanding he was about 25 years ahead of Dr Burr's experimental work. But in 1933, just as Dr Burr's work was moving into expression on the physical levels, Dr Ruth Drown comes along and demonstrates that it is possible to diagnose and treat at a distance, showing that a connection exists between practitioner and patient without any connecting wires, just using the energy field of the earth. This rather put radionics out ahead again, using techniques that were not capable of scientific proof. Then in the sixties Cleve Backster was able, through the use of a polygraph, to show that one body can act upon another at a distance. His work of eliciting reactions at a distance, ties in, as far as we can tell, with radionic broadcast techniques. The whole radionic technique of selecting healing ratios or rates generates a healing thought-form which is projected to the patient via an energy field, on the principle that energy follows thought.

Now the next step has been introduced into radionics by suggesting that man is not simply a plain electro-magnetic field, but that this field has force centres in it which govern the various organs of the body, and that it is through the balancing of these centres that health can be restored; it is a move away from the present complexity towards simplicity, toward, if you like, the prana of Indian theory and a more holistic approach to healing.

In a more esoteric vein the ancient teachings state that man is a spark of the Universal Mind and that the Universal Mind, as far as can be comprehended consists of seven vast planes of energy. These planes for convenience of expression form the systemic lines of latitude. Man in his totality is found upon the lowest of these, namely the cosmic physical plane.

Flowing through these seven latitudinal bands of energy or consciousness, are seven streams of energy which form the systemic lines of longitude. In the writings of Alice Bailey these seven longitudinal lines of energy are referred to as the Seven Rays. In the Bible they are called the Seven Spirits before the Throne of God. Each has its own qualities and characteristics which express themselves in and through man and the solar system he lives in.

Each of these vast energy fields form spheres one within another, rather after the style of the intricate Chinese carvings in which a series of ivory spheres move freely one within the other. Visualize if you will, seven great spheres of energy rotating in an east-west direction and within each of these, seven great spheres of colour rotating in a north-south direction and you will gain some inkling of the Field of Mind we live and move and have our being in.

This is of course extremely oversimplified and very theoretical, but there is plenty of literature on the subject from which the practitioner can glean knowledge which he will find useful in the practice of radionics. It is essential to have a basic understanding that mind is matter, and that matter is mind. Such a realization no doubt led Madame Blavatsky to state that matter was Spirit at its lowest level, and Spirit was matter at its highest level.

From the evidence available the ancient teachings equate the electro-dynamic field with the etheric body both of the planet and of man, and of all life-forms. Through this body they say, man is connected with the source of life. It sustains his physical organism and integrates him into the electro-dynamic field of the solar system. Now science, while accepting what Dr Burr has to say about the Life-field, would deny the existence of the etheric body as outlined in Eastern thought. But it is a curious fact that if one reads *Blueprint for Immortality* in the light of Eastern teachings about the etheric body, one sees immediately that both Dr Burr and the Indian teachers are speaking the same language, the parallels are constant and identical, both with strong philosophical implications.

The scientific community has for many years now been engaged in experimental work to explore the Life-fields. In recent years it became obvious that there was a direct correlation in their findings to Eastern thought, so much so that a certain number of scientists felt it was an embarrassment that should be got rid of, and in fact steps were taken to repudiate Burr's work. Caught with a smudge of 'esoteric lipstick' on their collar, what better way was there to deal with it than throw the shirt away? Fortunately Burr's theories are here to stay and a number of those who tried to oppose them have since concurred that there is more than a possibility that the theory of an etheric formative matrix may be a reality after all.

Given time, there can be little doubt that science will eventually recognize and confirm what the Eastern teachings have said for many thousands of years. Then we shall see many changes, amongst them a new medicine based on an understanding of these vital etheric energy fields and the natural laws that govern them. Sir James Mackenzie once said: 'The fact that medicine is becoming so complex implies that its study is being pursued on wrong lines; for a subject which is based on natural laws becomes easier to understand as the laws become better known.'

Radionics of course bases itself on natural laws and as a result is a relatively simple technique of healing which utilizes the etheric web or connective tissue of space for diagnostic and therapeutic purposes. In the chapters that follow I want to explore in some detail just how radionic practitioners can and do make use of the energy fields that surround us, and to show that in radionics lies the seed of a New Age healing art.

Chapter Three

THE GEOMETRIC ETHERIC LINK

'This spatial molecular chemistry (of Pasteur) is the direct ancestor of Watson and Cricks helical desoxyribose nucleic acid (DNA), one of the vital genetic building blocks of biological life – in its own essence a genetic formative force, with qualities reminiscent of those attributed by the ancients to their various spatial essences.'

> Fresh Evidence for a Biophysical Field.
> Drs G. Barnard and J. Stephenson

The content of this chapter was derived from experiences gained whilst using a radiesthetic chart for diagnosis at a distance. The same concepts apply to the use of radionic instruments and what follows is a slightly modified and updated version of an essay which appeared under the title of 'The Principle of Perception in Radiesthesia' in the June 1970 issue of the *Journal of the British Society of Dowsers*. Radionics basically is an instrumented form of radiesthesia; in both the practitioner dowses for imbalances or dis-ease in the energy fields of the patient.

One of the perennial questions familiar to every enquiring radiesthesist or radionic practitioner, is how does he register and perceive the impressions emitted by the patient at a distance? It is a question that has elicited, and in fact continues to elicit, a wide range of speculative and controversial answers. From these have arisen the physical and mental schools of thought regarding the dowsing phenomenon.

By its very nature perception is a difficult thing to explain. It is so simple that we take it for granted; so universal that every life form possesses it in varying degrees, and yet despite its immediacy, philosophers and scientists throughout the ages have written some of their most controversial works trying to explain what perception is.

It is important to recognize first that perception has two main facets, the subjective and the objective. The objective factors are easy to grasp as they entail speech, sight, touch and so forth. The common stuff of everyday experience derives from the objective world.

Through the narrowly tuned conscious reception faculties of the five senses, man has comprehended a singularly narrow spectrum of the surrounding environment. That which lies outside his immediate perception he ignorantly classifies as metaphysical.

Naturally it is the subjective aspect of perception that is difficult to discuss. There is no recognized terminology to express the very personal qualities of this aspect of perception. Also we are burdened with a heritage of mechanistic thought, which has succeeded in eliminating a variety of organic and human analogues from scientific explanation, and divorcing scientific theories about matter and action from metaphysics and theology.

Fortunately there are signs today indicating that individual scientists are strongly impelled to philosophize about the implications of their work, and we are seeing the first welcome glimmer of reconciliation between science and the true metaphysics of theology. Arthur Koestler has said – 'No honest scientist can now publish a book on physics without a metaphysical epilogue.'

In radionics we are primarily concerned with the subjective side of the perceptive process, so we begin with a distinct disadvantage whenever we attempt to theorize as to its nature.

Anyone who has seriously attempted to theorize in this field quickly realizes that conclusions based on strictly objective or subjective theories leave much to be desired. Obviously new explanatory concepts are required. But new concepts are drawn by analogy from some other conceptual system, and so we lean heavily upon physics to provide a comprehensive framework for our objective or physical explanation, and look to a variety of philosophies for the more esoteric modus operandi.

Personally I do not believe that a satisfactory explanation of the radionic phenomenon can be found in any theory based on a mental-physical dichotomy. Of necessity radionics is an expression of the inter-action of the objective and subjective realms, and for this reason any theory regarding its nature must take the middle path, and draw from both, those factors which by analog appear to form a holistic explanation of the phenomenon.

The original question regarding the perception of impressions from distant objects, immediately raises other factors which must fit into the mosaic of the answer if we are to obtain an overall picture.

What for instance is the nature of the force field wherein the radionic practitioner works? Is it simply an electro-magnetic field, or must we seek beyond the concept of a physical field to find the answer? And does that field in any way find its analogy within the human force field, which in certain aspects as we have seen is of an electro-magnetic nature; and if so, can we trace a reflection of the pattern in the link connecting the radionic practitioner with the

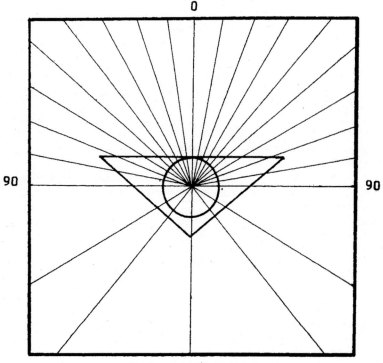

THE PSIONIC CHART

object of his enquiry, and in so doing throw some light on the subject of action at a distance? Naturally each question raises another, for the radiesthetic faculty in its multiple aspects, is an intrinsic quality of life.

My own theory regarding the linking phenomenon between patient and practitioner derives from a series of observable events related to the use of the psionic chart. Early in 1967 Dr Aubrey Westlake, author of *The Pattern of Health* which is a most excellent book dealing with the radiesthetic sense, gave me a copy of this chart which I began to use for diagnostic purposes.

When making a diagnosis with this chart the patient's blood spot is placed at the right-hand point of the triangle, and the Turenne witness which is an inert powder impregnated with the frequencies of a disease, is set on the left-hand point. Disease is read off as degrees of pendulum deviation from the mid-line marked zero.

In the process of selecting the correct homoeopathic similimum for the patient under analysis, the practitioner places the remedy or remedies at the downward pointing apex of the triangle. If the similimum is correct the pendulum swings away from the degrees of disease indicated and moves along the vertical mid-line of the chart, thus showing that the resonance of the disease has been cancelled out, and a balance of forces between the blood spot, the Turenne witness and the similimum has been established within the triangle.

Now the similimum is given to the patient, and if it works well enough to clear the disease from his system, then the practitioner upon checking his patient will similarly get a reading of zero along the mid-line of the chart.

I was immediately struck by the thought, that if the similimum placed on the triangle of the chart balances the forces therein, and the same reaction could be obtained after the patient had ingested the medicine, then there must be a triangle of force connecting the patient with the chart during an analysis. How else would a reading of zero be obtained?

I hope that this is clear, for my entire theory has emerged from this single observation. Subsequently, I have used the symbol of the triangle as a key to gain access to certain organic analogs, which I feel relate to the dowsing or radiesthetic phenomenon. Plato once said: 'Establish the triangle and the problem is two-thirds solved.' I feel very strongly that this axiom can be applied to the nature of perception in radionic diagnostic work and for that matter, to the action of healing at a distance by radionic means.

There are three factors which immediately concern us. The radionic practitioner or, when using the chart, the radiesthetist. The object sought after, which for our purposes is a patient undergoing a health analysis. And we are also concerned with the medium or force field they share in common with all life.

First the practitioner. Think of this individual in terms of energy. As an energy or force field subject to impressions, some of which register themselves via the five senses, and others which make their impact in a more subtle manner, but nevertheless involve the nervous system which is inextricably linked with the underlying force field.

The human force field as I have already mentioned has various aspects. The philosophical teachings of the East put forward the theory that objective form is but the outward manifestation of inner subjective energies . . . that there is nothing but energy and that it functions through a substance which inter-penetrates and activates all forms. They refer to this energy field as the etheric body, and state that it is positive to the negative physical form, that it galvanizes it into activity and acts as a cohesive force holding it together. Through it ALL sensations are received by the physical body.

Then of course there are the electro-dynamic aspects as outlined in the work of Dr Burr. It should be remembered too that experimental work has shown that the L-field can be modified and altered by the T or Thought-field, this is significant as far as the radionic practitioner is concerned.

Another aspect, even subtler than the electro-dynamic field of man, is the psi-field. The psi-field has been posited in order to construct theories regarding the phenomenon of precognition and extra sensory perception. These factors are now the focus of much intensive research and they must attract the attention of practitioners, for in an understanding of the psi-field and its possible relationship to the etheric body of Eastern speculative thought, we may well find clues leading to an explanation of radionic phenomenon.

Although the electro magnetic fields may be relevant to various aspects of radionics, my own theory is concerned with the more speculative elements of the etheric and psi-fields. Certain work with plants in America has shown conclusively that signals which lie beyond the electromagnetic spectrum, span distances irrespective of the more physical fields. I will cover this in more detail later on in the chapter.

Now we know that the radionic practitioner is able to perceive, that is to consciously or unconsciously register the impacts of various energies upon his system. This perception involves a basic principle of life, namely feedback. Feedback is that phenomenon in which the states of objects are coupled so that one object influences another.

The principle of feedback is applicable to the radionic process. For example the pattern of imbalance or disease in a patient influences the nervous system of the practitioner. This induction of disturbance via the psi-field reverberates through the nervous system temporarily altering its pattern.

Anatomically there is a sensory input mechanism. Through the simple reflex arc the receptors of the nervous system pass the registered impact of energy, via the central nervous system to the effectors. The motor output activates muscle and the pendulum is impelled to move. This of course is one explanation, there are others. Wilhelm Reich for example put forward the theory that the dowsing reaction occurred when the orgone field of the dowser reacted with

the orgone field of the water or object sought after. Clearly something of this nature does happen when dowsing for water, frequently
if the dowser tries to stop the willow or hazel rod from bending up or
down as the case may be, the rod will still turn in his hands with such
force as to strip the bark from the rod. Here there is firm evidence to
suggest that one force field acts upon another. When diagnosing
through radionic means it seems that the nervous and muscular
systems are directly involved.

Without going into details regarding the transmission of nerve
impulses, it is important to bear in mind that the accurate modula-
tion and control of nerve impulses is governed by a host of RNA
(ribonucleic acid), proteins and transmitter substances, all made
under the direction of the DNA (deoxyribonucleic acid), and that
DNA, the storehouse of genetic information, may ultimately act as
the pattern maker of cognition, memory and thought. Three important factors in radionic processes.

Your attention is called to the fact that DNA plays a role in modu-
lating neural patterns, firstly because the molecular double helix configuration of DNA is peculiarly related to the symbol of the triangle,
and secondly because I intend to use the DNA analog and relevant
protein structures for the elaboration of a functional geometrical
pattern of the psi-field.

When the practitioner puts the questions during the course of a
diagnosis, we can assume that the brain acts as a step up transformer
of the impulse received. It is possible that the brain acts as an ampli-
fying system with its neurons functioning like transistors. In electronic terms there could be an amplification of impression with little
distortion of the original signal content. Chemically this would be
conditioned by the oxygen atoms of the amino acid acetycholine-
esterase, which regulates the movements of the electrically charged
atoms in the membranes of nerve fibres, which in turn mediate the
electrical communication currents of activated nerve cells, creating
as previously mentioned, muscular response and pendulum movement.

Relative to the brain as an amplifier is Marshall's theory of ESP
as holistic resonance. He states that the transmission of information
between two points separated in space, without the intervention of a
physical signal, involves the reproduction of a particular pattern of
neural activity in one human, analogous to that in another human.

A similar reaction occurs during a radionic or radiesthetic diagnosis. The practitioner sets up a pattern of neural activity by mentally positing the question, is such and such a disease present in the
patient? He stabilizes this pattern with the presence of a Turenne

witness, or in the case of radionics by placing a numerical value known as a 'rate' or 'ratio' on the dials of the instrument.

If the disease pattern is present in the patient, then no matter at what distance from the practitioner that patient is, a resonance is set up between its vibratory quality and the vibratory quality of the practitioner's enquiry, and he gets a positive response from the pendulum. Incidentally this factor points out the need for absolutely clear and concise questioning in any radiesthetic or radionic work.

If the question is not clearly formulated and directed, then a short circuiting in the feedback process seems to occur and something within the practitioner answers with a positive response to the image contained within his own mind, and he gets, in most instances an incorrect reaction. This can occur easily when fatigue is present, or when outside influences disturb the concise formulation and projection of the resonant thought image. Relative to the field affecting field concept, there is the experience of the Abbe Mermet, one of the world's most experienced dowsers in his day. He took time out to show some school children how to dowse for water but no matter how hard he tried he could get no reaction with his pendulum. He commented that there must be some great disturbance in the earth's magnetic field for this to have happened. The next day news was received that at that time a tidal wave had hit Japan.

In 1661 Joseph Glanville compared the communication of two minds to the communication of a sound between resonant strings, and concluded that motions in the brain may be transmitted through the ether as sounds through air. His concept bears a striking resemblance to the more modern theory of Marshall.

There is an ancient axiom which states that 'Energy follows Thought'. Paracelsus was never reluctant to point out that the human body can act at a distance while remaining at rest in one place, and that nothing must be attributed to the body itself, but only to the forces which flow from it.

Dr Borchard in an article entitled 'The Human Body when Dowsing', published in the December 1967 issue of the BSD Journal wrote: 'I believe that in dowsing something goes out of the dowser'. May I suggest that what goes out of the dowser is in fact the resonant image of thought, and that the bonding or mating of that resonant image to the resonance of the object sought after, succeeds in bringing perception of that object or quality to the practitioner via sensory incursion of his psi-field followed by automatic neural response.

The effect of thought over distances has been demonstrated by Cleve Backster, director of the Backster Research Foundation in New York. Nearly everyone is now familiar with the fact that he has found that by employing a polygraph normally used to test emotional stimulation in human subjects, that plants register apprehension, fear, pleasure and relief. A series of experiments was conducted which revealed that plants responded not only to overt threats to their well being, but even more remarkably, to the feelings and intentions of the living creatures, animals as well as human, with whom they were closely associated.

Under experimental conditions Backster employed the polygraphists standard 'threat to well being' test. In his mind he decided to burn the plant; the plant's reaction to his thought was so strong as to cause the tracing pen to leap across the graph paper. Similarly plants have reacted to the tensions of people under stress, and registered the signals from dying cells in the drying blood of an accidentally cut finger. What is more they are able to receive signals over a considerable distance, for they have registered Mr Backster's intention to return to his office from over fifteen miles away. Backster reports that he tried unsuccessfully to block out whatever signals the plants were receiving by using a Faraday cage and lead lined containers. Still communication continued, so it seems that the signal may not fall within the known electro-dynamic spectrum.

Subsequently I have had the pleasure of many conversations with Cleve Backster relative to his work and there is clearly contained in it evidence that can be used to explain certain radionic phenomena. I have also spent many hours working with Dr Marcel Vogel, senior research chemist for IBM, San Jose, California. His work with man-plant communication methods has really outstanding merit and shows clearly the effect of thought spanning great distances. Here is one example.

In 1973 Dr Vogel lectured at the First International Congress of Parapsychology and Psychotronics which was held in Prague. He took advantage at this time to run an experiment involving the impact of thought at a distance. In San Jose some six thousand miles away Dr Ward Lamb spent fifteen minutes on two consecutive evenings at an agreed time, tuned into the plant and the electronic equipment attached to it. In Prague Dr Vogel concentrated during this same period and at intervals projected powerful bursts of thought at the heart chakra of Dr Lamb. On the first evening the graph showed three distinct responses to these projections of thought. On the second evening there was no response in San Jose at all and Dr Lamb was under the impression that the experiment had failed. What in fact had happened is that Dr Vogel after a tiring day of lecturing had fallen asleep and had not in fact projected any thought to Dr Lamb. The experiment had in fact been a great success and is one that is of much significance to radionics.

Both Backster and Vogel have established in their experimentation that plants are sentient; and that they have a definite and sympathetic response to what happens to other living things within their environment. Secondly they indicate that action at a distance, long ascribed to gravitational forces originating in planets, is in fact a feature of a non-material field. These findings are causing scientists to assume the existence of another universal energy field, unique to life, in which sentience is a feature. This certainly tallies with the etheric web of the earth and to the connective etheric tissue of space.

To the radionic practitioner who uses broadcasting techniques, action at a distance is an everyday phenomena. To the more orthodox thinker such techniques must seem rather suspect, yet in the sixteenth and seventeenth centuries the sympathetic cure of wounds was a well authenticated happening.

In his *Sylva Sylvarum*, published in 1672, Francis Bacon writes: 'It is constantly received and avouched, that the anointing of the weapon that maketh the wound, will heal the wound itself.' He goes on to describe the preparation of an ointment, and the various tests to which the practice has been subjected, all of which seem to show that the cure is obtained only when the ointment is applied to the weapon and not to the wound, that the weapon may be at a great distance, and that the cure does not depend on the patient knowing of the anointing.

Sir Kenelm Digby has a version of the cure in which a cloth covered with blood from the wound is soaked in a solution of the 'Powder of Sympathy' (specially prepared iron sulphate). Glanville asserted that the cure of wounds at a distance had been put out of all doubt by the noble Sir Digby.

Scientists today are not so readily convinced but mention of a cure also occurs in Spratt's *History of the Royal Society*. The writer remarks that a reported effect on wounds of a certain poison from Macassar which touches the blood from the wound, is not strange to those who study sympathy.

Diagnosis and treatment at a distance are both inevitably related to thought; in fact I contend that without the directive power of thought no cure would be effected. It is the energy which follows thought that brings the curative power of the selected remedy or ratio to bear upon the patient. If thought had no part, then any lock of hair left on the floor of the barber's shop, would subject us to a wide range of influences, and we would find ourselves reacting to a random bombardment of uncomfortable sensations. This fortunately for us does not happen.

Having considered the practitioner as a complexity of energy fields which are integrated into the energy field of the earth, and theorized as to the role of thought and resonant images in the phenomenon of feedback between practitioner and patient, we can now proceed to explore and elaborate on the nature of the link between them, outlining the reciprocal interplay of energies and constructing a model of the functional geometric nature of the psi-field.

Our knowledge of the relationship between man and the spectrum of surrounding and penetrating forces, small as it is, demands that in postulating a force field through which the practitioner works, that such a field must be appropriate to the nature and behaviour of the protoplasmic cell.

According to Professor Oliver Reiser of the University of Pittsburgh, the archetypal pattern of the DNA double-helix is an expression of a cosmic field of energy which in some way is the guide to biological evolution. Rudolf Steiner speaks of the etheric formative forces in this role, and it is clear that one may find clues as to the nature of the invisible force field underlying matter, by studying the geometry of the precipitated forms, particularly the structuring of DNA and certain protein complexes.

The psionic chart gives us a clue. The merit of any chart used for diagnostic purposes in medical radiesthesia lies in its inherent structural conformity to the pattern and laws of the energy field in which it is designed to function. The psionic chart is a graphic example of combined, symbolic geometric forms that key themselves to the patterns emerging from the etheric formative forces.

Such conformity to the fundamental structural expressions of the paraphysical levels of matter make this chart uniquely suitable for work in medical radiesthesia, providing an ideal focal point through which an interplay of energies can manifest, revealing even the subtlest imprints of disease upon the human Life-field.

Carlyle once wrote: 'In a symbol lies concealment of revelation'. This has been the contention of wise men for many centuries past, and we are seeing the ever increasing use of symbols in the technocracy of today for the simple reason that a single symbol has the capacity to represent a vast amount of information, to contain it in the smallest possible space, and make it available at a moment's notice. The symbol is in fact Nature's expression of economy and effectiveness; understood and applied correctly it will reveal to the radionic practitioner a profound insight into his work.

The psionic chart as we can see is composed of three basic geometric symbols of specific dimensions. From a symbolic standpoint the square can be said to represent the personality (low self) or 'the city which stands four-square'. In other words the combined energies of the physical, etheric, emotional and mental force fields.

The circle has ever been the Symbol of the centres of power within the etheric field, and it is contained within the downward pointing triangle which represents material and involutionary activity. There can be no doubt that such a combination of geometric symbols make the psionic chart an excellent tool for exploring energy relationships in health and disease.

Of the symbols incorporated into the chart, the triangle is perhaps the most revealing. As previously mentioned there occurs a balancing of forces within the triangle when the correct similimum has been found for the patient. This phenomenon, and the subsequent readings of zero, following successful elimination of the disease from oral ingestion of the remedy, strongly suggest that the patient is subjectively linked to the chart by way of a symbolic triangle of energy. Later we shall see that the downward pointing triangle of the chart is in fact overshadowed by yet another subjective triangle, thus completing the symbol of the link existing between patient and practitioner.

Having put the hypothesis forward that patient and practitioner are geometrically linked during a radiesthetic diagnosis, I should now like to explore the possible reciprocal interplay of energies between them, which in the final analysis give a penetrating summary of the patient's state of health.

Initially I will trace the hypothetical energy exchange within the confines of the symbol, and later, relative to the whole psi-field.

First we must understand that each triangle is basically the expression of one fundamental energy and two secondary forces. The fundamental energy at the apex of each triangle is emanative by nature, and the two secondary points, one at each end of the common base line, are receptive. Strictly speaking all points shift from emanative to receptive and back again during diagnostic work. All have a variety of qualities, but for purposes of clarity each point will be designated in a certain manner.

Now let us consider each point more closely. The point at the apex of the upward pointing triangle represents the patient who acts as an EMANATIVE centre of energy, giving off a continual stream of qualified energies into the surrounding psi-field. By qualified energies I mean those energies that reflect the mental, emotional and physical states of the patient under consideration.

The second point, located at the left end of the base line, is a receptive force centre which is EVOCATIVE by nature. This is represented on the physical level by any one of the Turenne disease or organ witnesses.

The third point at the right-hand end of the base line is a MAGNE-TIC centre of force wherein the grounding of the emanating energy from the patient is completed. This is represented by the patient's sample, be it a blood spot or a snippet of hair.

The fourth and lower point is designated as a DISTRIBUTIVE centre, and is in fact one of the positive centres of force or a chakra within the Life-field of the practitioner.

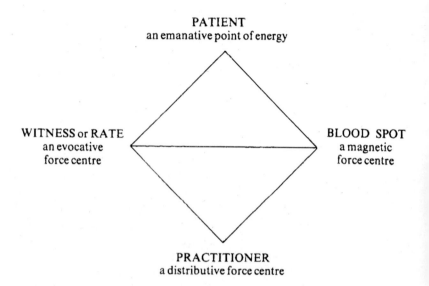

PATIENT
an emanative point of energy

WITNESS or RATE
an evocative
force centre

BLOOD SPOT
a magnetic
force centre

PRACTITIONER
a distributive force centre

So now we have the following diamond shaped symbol represent-ing the link between patient and practitioner.

The practitioner, by mentally asking if a certain disease is present within the patient, links himself via the Turenne witness and blood spot, to the patient, giving the following flow pattern of energy.

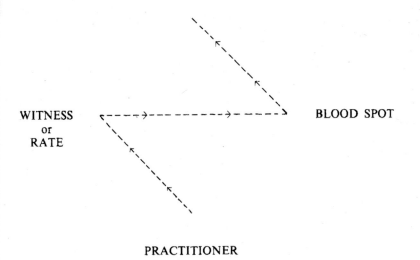

If the disease as represented by the witness (or in radionics the rate or ratio) and the resonant image within the mind of the dowser, is acutally present within the patient, the process of feedback through the intervening psi-field is instantaneous.

A synthesis occurs between the emanated vibratory force of the disease and the evocative force of the witness. They blend to form a point of qualified energy. This point of qualified energy now reacts with the blood spot or magnetic centre which is vitally responsive to the evocative force of the Turenne witness. This sets up an interplay of forces between the two points of the base line.

This interplay of forces is registered in the psi-field of the practitioner and is distributed via his nervous system, creating an imbalance which results in the involuntary muscular movements which impel the pendulum into activity, thus measuring off the degree of disease present in the patient.

Diagramatically this would give the following pattern of energy flow.

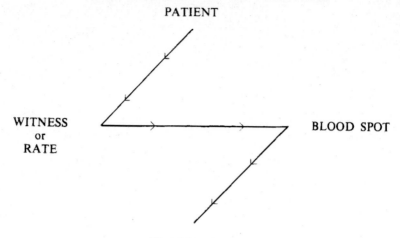

By combining the two patterns of energy flow a diamond shaped symbol made up of two triangles becomes representational of the link between patient and practitioner.

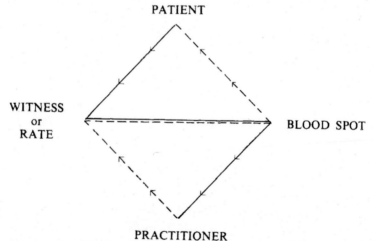

Relative to this I would like to quote a paragraph from *Esoteric Astrology* by Alice Bailey:

'This diamond shaped formation of the inter-related energies is the proto-typal pattern which lies behind the etheric network and is its final conditioning influence as far as our earth is concerned.'

The diamond symbol then is a single unit of the psi-field. By taking its pattern and extending it into a multi-dimensional network, it forms, in theory at least, a vast geometrically structured force field that permeates space.

Each line is potentially positive and negative, and each confluence of lines contains the potential of emanative, evocative, magnetic and distributive qualities. The illustration is drawn on a single plane in order to keep it as simple as possible, but it should be visualized to extend in all dimensions and directions to form a field which surrounds and inter-penetrates the earth and all forms upon it.

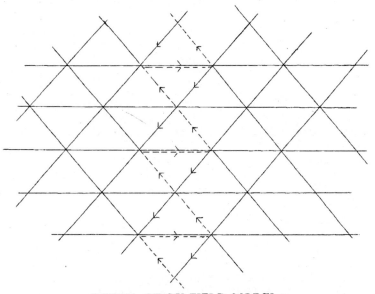

DETAIL OF PSI-FIELD MODEL

An area where this energy pattern has been utilized in a practical manner, is architecture. Buckminster Fuller has made full use of this fact in Nature to develop one of the strongest and most economical structural units known to man, namely the triangular sections of the geodesic dome. As you can see the pattern of the psi-field coincides with those of geodesic domes.

Fuller states that the mathematical patterning and inter-transformability of Nature's geometric structurings are the only reality of the universe, and that in any network, high energy charges refuse to take the long way round to their opposite pole. They tend to push through the separating space. Thus energy will automatically triangulate via the diagonal of a square, or via the triangulating di-agonals of any other polygon to which force is applied. Triangular systems, he says, represent the shortest most economical network of energy. Consider how closely this ties in with the etheric network of the earth and its use in radionic diagnosis and treatment.

By positing a triangular structured psi-field, the theory can be ac-commodated within the framework of existing physical language and thought, and at the same time conform to the speculative theo-ries of Ancient India relative to the etheric force field which underlies all creation.

In 1956 at the CIBA Foundation Symposium on Extrasensory Perception, G. D. Wassermann, in his paper entitled 'An Outline of a Field Theory of Organismic Form and Behaviour', put forward suggestions regarding the nature of the psi-field using a quantum field theory. He claimed to have overcome some of the difficulties of a field interpretation of psi phenomena, by constructing a cascade process of fields in which no attenuation with distance occurs, and he assumes that although energy is required by psi-fields, their inter-action with ordinary matter fields is absent or extremely small, so that psi-fields can be propagated over long distances without absorp-tion.

More recent theories from Russian scientists, and the evidence of Cleve Backster's and Marcel Vogel's work with plant perception, all point to the fact that anyone dealing with psi phenomena, and theo-rizing about the transmission and reception of information over dis-tances, as occurs in radionic practice, is going to have to seek beyond the known electromagnetic fields in order to find answers to the problems this phenomena poses.

The difficulty of understanding the problems of emitters and recei-vers may be overcome by recognizing that there are certain physio-logical and neurological functions with which the psi-field interacts, and that thought plays a very potent role in this reciprocal action.

Man is a complex field of energies submerged in the energy field of the earth. At conception and throughout life the atoms of his body are derived from the earth, and according to Eastern thought the substance of his etheric force field is derived from the etheric body of the planet. In the physical cell then we should see a reflection of the archetypal pattern of the etheric web that constitutes his Life-field, and that in turn should reflect the pattern of the energy field in which he is totally immersed.

The Hermetic axiom: 'As above, so below' clearly indicates that the Ancients were of the opinion that the microcosm (man) con-tained the patterns of the macrocosm (cosmic man). Today we may find it a bit difficult to understand the veiled symbolism and techniques of investigation used by these people, but it is possible to find remarkable organic analogs in the human body which reflect the patterning of the underlying force fields.

For example, collagen the main supportive protein of connective tissue, is found throughout the animal kingdom. Nature, as C. Smith points out in his book *Molecular Biology*, having hit upon the means of conferring tensile strength, has never been able to better it. Collagen then, pervades all animal forms, just as the etheric web pervades the universe like a connective tissue of space. It has as already mentioned, tremendous tensile strength, just like the geodesic domes designed by Buckminster Fuller.

One means of studying the structure of collagen which has a simple amino-acid constitution consisting mainly of glycine and proline, is the study of the synthetic poly-peptides such as polyglycine and polyproline. The patterning of polyglycine exhibits the diamond shape structuring of the psi-field model, fitting with ease into the pattern when illustrated as follows.

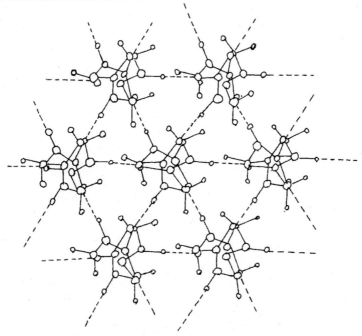

SKETCH OF POLYGLYCINE 2 VIEWED END ON
All chemical symbols are omitted in order not to complicate the drawing

A modification of the diamond structure of the archetypal pattern also demonstrates itself in the double-helix configuration of the DNA molecule. Once again this is a pattern common to all living things from unicellular organisms to man.

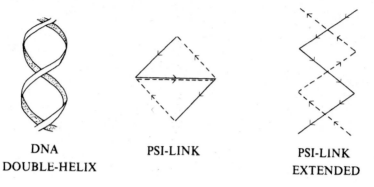

DNA
DOUBLE-HELIX

PSI-LINK

PSI-LINK
EXTENDED

At first sight one might say that the link pattern does not conform to the DNA double-helix, but provided we can accept the analogy in its broadest principles, and are not too mechanistic in our thinking, one is able to observe that it does. Rather than attempt mental gymnastics it is simpler to make a paper model of the link, which if grasped at its top and bottom points, will upon stretching form a double-helix configuration.

There is evidence enough now for scientists to assert that the two chains of the double-helix are of opposite polarity. The sequence of atoms in one chain running in the opposite direction to that of the other chain. Similarly the flow of energy in the links of the psi-field are seen to flow in opposite directions, and may if one chooses, be said to have opposite polarity. This applies also to the parallel chains of the links throughout the field. Quite a series of coincidental similarities.

The pattern of the link also appears in meiotic cell division, the chromosomes arranging themselves into helices. More remarkable still is the pattern formed when the spindle fibres connect the centromeres to the centrioles. The centromeres at this stage have divided, and the chromosomes are moving to opposite poles of the cell. The illustration shows the close similarity to the psi-link pattern.

I am drawn again to quote from Dr Borchard's article on the human body when dowsing. She writes: 'I believe that dowsing obeys the very same law that governs the formation of the living organism; both its growth and its functioning.' And again. 'It is really, the force we dealt with before, the middle power between the opposite poles.'

Here she speaks of polarity as the governing or principle force in dowsing. If we consider once again the symbol of the psi-link, and the play of forces along the common base line of both triangles, it is evident that this displays the 'middlepower' of polarity between the opposite poles – between practioner and patient.

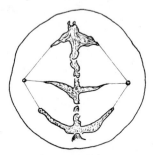

SIXTH STAGE OF MEIOTIC DIVISION

I hope to have shown that it is essential to formulate a field theory based on observable phenomena, if we are to obtain a deeper understanding of our work relative to perception in radionics and radiesthesia. By analog to the molecular configuration of certain protein substances and DNA, it is possible to build such a theory relative to the geometric structuring of the psi-field – a theory which relates the patterning in the cell to those patterns of the formative forces of the cosmos.

The principle of perception in radiesthesia and radionics lies quite simply in the polarization of the psi-field, by the introduction into that field of a clear concise resonant thought pattern. The bonding of that pattern to a similar pattern in the patient at a distance, brings perception of that particular disease to the practitioner.

If I seem to have dwelt unduly upon the structure of the psi-field, it is because I do not see the radionic force as traversing space in some indeterminate manner, but according to certain principles and laws pertaining to the action of thought upon the etheric body of the earth. These etheric threads, these beams of light can be activated by thought and used as a connecting link between the practitioner and his patient, they are ultra-microscopically small, their triangular formation having a direct analog to the structure of the DNA double-helix, they are the formative-field we live in. The Kahuna priests of Polynesia utilized these energy lines to heal people at a distance, they referred to them as the aka thread, and said that through an act of will on the part of the healer, energies of a healing nature could be directed along the aka thread to the patient, so we see the idea of a link between healer and patient is not a new concept by any means. However in the light of modern knowledge in the field of physiology it is possible to theorize about the structural formation of these threads and perhaps from this new ideas will arise.

Certainly an understanding of energy fields, be they electromagnetic, biophysical, Life-fields, T-fields, etheric or psi-fields, is essential to the radionic practitioner for a fuller and deeper understanding of his work.

Chapter Four

RADIONIC ETHERIC
PHOTOGRAPHY

'Does it mean anything to you when I say that electricity and photography are closely related because the human being is electrical in origin
and nature? This must be demonstrated on the physical plane by the aid
of the needed sensitive apparatus.'

Esoteric Healing, Alice A. Bailey (Feb. 1944)

From the evidence available it is clearly possible to photograph the
force fields and energies that are utilized in radionics. The chiropractor Dr Ruth Drown was the first to do this, producing some
very remarkable pictures with what she called her Radio-Vision
instrument, much of this work was carried out in California in the
1930's.

Ruth Drown theorized that there is a vital fluid-like Life Force
which flows through the entire universe, energizing and expressing
itself through all forms, each having a different rate of vibration thus
giving rise to certain elements and substances from which the material world was built.

She spoke of a fluid in the thalamus which is said to give balance
to the head, rather like the bubble in a spirit-level. That fluid, she
claimed, was also a form of liquid light, a condensation of the ani-
mating Life Force. She went on to say that it was to be found in the
blood plasma and bathing the entire nervous system, entering by
way of the pineal gland and terminating in the Bundle of His in the
heart.

The photographs made with her Radio-Vision instrument were
obtained by directly attaching the individual to the instrument by
wire leads or by placing a blood spot at a point in the circuitary. The
patient's energy then flowed into the instrument, rates were set up
on the dials of the instrument in order to select the area to be photographed, and the selected energy from the patient then flowed across
the emulsion of the film. No light as we understand it touched the

41

photographic plate, simply the light of the Life Force. One photograph of the nucleus of the cranial nerves taken with the instrument
revealed the form of a lotus leaf deep in the cortex of the brain.

She was at a loss to understand why people could not comprehend
that the invisible Light was the activating means which produced the
pictures. To her it was quite clear and she expressed her understanding in these words.

'The fact that some of our radio-vision pictures are taken by using the
blood as a "radio beam" is explained in this manner: when placed on a
blotter, the blood is crystallized, even as ice is crystallized steam, and each
small atom is the precipitated crystallized end of an invisible line which
reaches into the ethers. This invisible line passes through the body over the
nerves and through the blood vessels, and the electrons from air, water
and earth supply the body structure, attaching themselves to that line,
which holds the pattern of the body.

The invisible line is therefore the Life Force of the body. It also takes the
form of liquids and gases when the electronic flow is speeded up fast
enough to produce heat. When the body ceases to be animated by this Life
Force – in other words, when death comes – we cannot tune in to it with
our instruments. The Life Force or "radio beam" has been withdrawn.

Since the blood is crystallized light, it acts as light and has the speed of
light. Therefore its energy passes around the world seven and three-
quarter times per second, possibly more. This does away with the idea of
distance, and shows that the vibration of everything in the world is *where
we are*; we need only take this vibration out of the ethers and pass it
through our instrument in order either to treat a patient at a distance or
make a picture of any portion of his body.'

She goes on to say:

'In our work we are unable to take a picture of anyone under an anaesthetic. The reason for this is that when a patient is under anaesthetic, the
mental body is forced out of the physical (that is why there is no feeling in
the physical body at such times), and the former stands to one side. In
order to bring the mental body back enough so that it can outline the picture, we must use a certain kind of homoeopathic remedy with the
patient's vibration.'

Dr Drown's explanation of how the radionic photographs were
obtained is far from scientific, but there are a number of statements
which bear some thinking about. For example the implication that in
a spot of blood are the frequency patterns of any part of the human
body, and that those patterns of energy are present at all times any
where on earth and can be identified and photographed just by tuning
into them through the appropriate radionic instruments. It is interesting too that radionic photographs could not be obtained by her of

a person under anaesthetic, unless a certain (unspecified) homoeopathic remedy was used to create some link between the bodies separated out by the anaesthetic. Homoeopathic remedies are of course in the main pure energy particularly above the potency of 12c. Perhaps the remedy provided the 'radio beam' required to obtain the pictures in cases like this.

It is my good fortune to possess a number of excellent radio-vision photographs taken personally by Dr Drown during the 1930's. When I first got them some years ago I must confess that I took one look at them, read the diagnostic interpretation of each which unfortunately to me did not make too much sense, so they lay in the files until I met Dr Dennis Milner of Birmingham University and had an opportunity to listen to him lecture and see his remarkable slides of the etheric formative forces which he, Ted Smart and their assistant Brian Meredith had taken. I immediately saw a parallel in the Drown photos, it was simply a matter of interpreting them in terms of the etheric forces instead of pictures of pathological conditions. I am sure that the Drown pictures can be interpreted as parts of the body evidencing pathological changes, it is just that unless one has been trained what to look for, as one would have to be for example in X-ray interpretation, then there is no way of knowing what one is looking at. This is in complete contrast of course to the radionic photographs taken at the de la Warr Laboratories; in these the organs are clearly seen.

Ruth Drown obviously had this criticism levelled at her for she wrote:

> 'The statement has been made that in our photographs cellular structure is unlike any shown in the histological slides under a microscope. These pictures are obtained from the actual living tissues of the body, which are different from those that have been removed from the body, as seen under the microscope. The cells in the live body have a tone and life activity that does not exist in the same structure, once it has been removed from the body.
>
> It is true that our approach to this subject differs from the methods heretofore used; nevertheless, the time has come when the doctor must learn more about the animating Life Force of the patient and its many variables than about the mere functions of the body.'

Her response to criticism is fair enough, we cannot really know what human tissues look like when functioning with no outside interference to the body; tissue excised has lost its Life Force so it cannot truly represent the live form. The remarkable thing is, and Ruth Drown could not have known this when she did her photographic work in the 1930's, that histological pictures taken with electron microscopes in the modern laboratories of today have a striking and direct resembalance to her own pictures. Certain pictures taken by her of the energy fields of the brain are literally identical to modern microscopic studies.

Certainly the last paragraph of her statement has a piercing and one hopes a prophetic ring to it. There can be little doubt that when orthodox medicine recognizes these etheric Life-Fields a revolution will come about that will transform medical practice and make it more effective. The indiscriminate use of crude drugs will go by the board, and the causes of disease will be sought out in the pre-physical areas of matter and treated constructively rather than through suppression of symptom patterns by drugs or surgery.

A number of Radio-Vision photographs taken by Ruth Drown are here included along with the diagnostic interpretation. They are well worth comparing with histological pictures in any good book on the study of cells. They can also be looked at from the point of view that they express the patterns of the etheric formative forces; look at the vast sweeps of energy across the emulsion, note the circular disc-like shapes of the warmth ether that even appear to cast shadows. These are remarkable evidence of the forces that lie beyond the range of our five senses, and they confirm the fact that it is possible to photograph them with a radionic instrument that does not utilize light to get an image on to the film, but the energy of the Life-Force itself which contains Light of another kind.

Many of Drown's pictures were taken before panels of eminent medical doctors, who saw in them one of the dreams of medical science come true . . . the visual evidence on film of cross sections of soft tissue structures as they existed in the living body. Over the years many of the findings in the Radio-Vision pictures have been verified by post-mortem surgery, thus proving the efficacy of the technology that produced them.

Drown said that scientists outside the medical field should recognize the great potential that this radionic technique holds. That it could be used in the fields of mineral prospecting, agriculture, nuclear physics and space technology. It is recorded that she took a photograph with her radionic instrument of the astronauts in space, using their newspaper picture as a witness instead of blood crystals.

Ruth Drown wrote:

'New research is carrying this work to a higher plane of achievement, with no end in sight to what may be recorded by these methods. New designs in the instruments, moving constantly towards even *simpler* arrangements are revealing ways to tap into cosmic laws and secrets never hitherto accessible to man. Special sensitized materials and devices open incredible new vistas for the human race.'

Then she added this thought:

'Everything is *here, now*. All we have to do is tune in on it.'

Abrams, although he did not use any form of instrumentation in his attempts to photograph what he referred to as psychic energies, did succeed in getting images on film. He records however that these images were so faint as not to be suitable for reproduction.

In his experiments he found that individuals with a capacity to discharge spontaneously large amounts of energy, could record an image on film of this discharge. Sensitive film wrapped in black paper was held near the forehead of the subject for a period of 30 seconds to five minutes. The energy discharge was augmented by placing a strip of red material across the head and the action of the psychic rays intensified by interposing a strip of aluminium between the plate and the forehead of the individual. A coating of shellac or insulating tape was found to obstruct the energy flow.

Abrams said that his experiments did not refer to thought forms, and his pictures, which he called psychograms, were simply the recorded images of energy discharge. One cannot help wondering if his subjects had been asked to project mentally, a clear and concentrated thought form, that he might have got better pictures. It is evident that they were discharging energy through the ajna or brow chakra onto the film held near the forehead, now this chakra, when functioning properly has the capacity to discharge, project and direct thought forms over any distance, certainly it can be used to impress an image on sensitive film, and I think that one can see an example of this type of activity expressed in the pictures taken by Ted Serios. It is worth adding too, that the ajna chakra is the centre of the low-self or personality and if used and stimulated in an excessive way, for example in many repeated attempts to get images on film then one can fairly accurately predict that personality disorders will occur as a result of such over stimulation. It is a matter to be approached with care; one may speculate that photographing through the use of a radionic camera serves to act as a buffer to ill effects.

The late George de la Warr, his wife Marjorie and their assistant Leonard Corte, took up the investigation of radionic photography at the De La Warr Laboratories in Oxford during the 1950's. New cameras were devised and developed and pictures of a completely different nature were obtained. Organs were clearly defined, areas of pathology stood out sharply; in short the pictures were recognizable as physical structures and far more easy to interpret.

De La Warr wrote of this work in a News Letter saying:

'In my experience with our Radionic Camera the presence of a magnetic field indicates the presence of etheric energy. The magnetic fields of nature are completely suffused with the energy patterns of the etheric counterpart. If we consider a simple plant, for instance, we know it is suffused with an etheric counterpart of the plant appropriate to the stage of its life cycle.'

So it was clear that the radionic photographs that were being obtained were etheric in nature.

Some 12,000 radionic photographs were taken at the laboratories. Scientists investigated the de la Warr's claims. Some were sympathetic many were not and it was found that if a person who was hostile to the concepts of radionic photography was present at a photographic session, that no images could be obtained. Imagine the delight of the sceptic and the consternation of the team at the labs. This temperamental aspect of the camera led many a scientist to reject out of hand any evidence produced by it. There were of course those who were sympathetic and could obtain pictures from the camera. It must induce a sense of wonder in the open minded individual to attempt to photograph the energy field of tablets containing a homoeopathic potency of Aconitum, and then see a picture of the flowers of this plant clearly impressed upon the emulsion of the plate. I have seen these plates, they not only have images, but those images are etched right into the emulsion as though they had been cut out by some invisible force.

No doubt one day radionic photographic techniques will play an important role in many fields of human endeavour, especially in the field of healing. The present drawback is that only certain people can obtain images on film whilst using the radionic camera. Why, it is not entirely clear, but the theory is that those who can obtain pictures have a certain quality to their own Life-field which sensitises and charges the plate with an undetermined type of energy. When this happens, and it does quite spontaneously, then images are obtained.

Recently in June of this year (1974) I took Dr Marcel Vogel who was visiting with us from California, down to Burford in Oxfordshire to the home of Miss Elizabeth Baerlein and Mrs Lavender Dower. They have a de la Warr radionic camera which fifteen years ago produced several thousand pictures, at that time they worked with a person who could sensitise the plates.

Since then they have made any number of attempts to get pictures but with no results. I have tried myself but to no avail. Dr Vogel having familiarized himself with the equipment showed them a technique of charging the plates. A number of runs were made with curious results, some plates showing the all too familiar lack of exposure, others with no exposure to light at all coming out completely black. Out of a morning's work two plates showed a discernible image, plates on which Mrs Dower and Miss Baerlein had endeavoured to photograph Dr Vogel's heart chakra. The images were there but they looked identical to Ruth Drown's radio-vision pictures, it was rather a turn up for the books to get Drown-like images on a de la Warr camera.

It should be emphasized that these plates were charged and sensitized by a method made known to them by Dr Vogel. He did not charge the plates himself but imparted the technique, so that at future sessions the pictures could be taken without him being present. It was an exciting prospect because if this method worked for anybody then it would be possible to run a whole new series of radionic pictures. Subsequent runs have resulted in a blank, no exposures at all even though this new technique looked so promising. It is obvious now that the very presence of Dr Vogel was sufficient to sensitize the plates, although he did not touch them or make any conscious effort to charge them himself. So in effect it is back to square one until such time as an operator is found who has the ability to charge and sensitize the plates sufficiently to get pictures.

In my collection of radionic photographs is an original picture. On the back is written . . . Radiesthetic picture of Rectal Fistula taken by Miss E. Maxwell-Moore and Mrs E. Shippard on the camera designed and built by them in 1956. Accompanying the picture is the following description.

Explanation of this radionic photograph:

'The patient was an elderly man who had had an operation for haemorrhoids some years before. He complained to his surgeon of great pain, and thought it was a recurrence of his original condition. The surgeon informed him that there was nothing wrong except some bruising caused by riding. A radionic practitioner analyzed the condition as a rectal fistula. The analysis was confirmed by this photograph. The rectal muscle can be clearly seen in the photograph. The fistula itself can be seen as a small white ball, and the radiations from it can be seen spreading to cause inflammation. The ball of apparent light enclosing the condition is an actual photograph of the radiesthetic force attacking the diseased part to effect a cure. It is interesting to note that you can also see the buckle of the patient's belt quite clearly. The patient was about 200 miles from the camera when the photograph was taken. The patient made a complete and rapid recovery.

The apparatus consisted of a good camera enclosed in certain contrivances worked out by the practitioner, and the photograph was taken on Kodak roll film. For development and printing the film was sent to a photographic firm at Hastings by post and returned after processing. The camera did the same for another practitioner, who provided the film, loaded the camera, took his own photographs and had them commercially processed. The camera was then dismantled as it was not found to be of any practical value.'

I have given this description in full because really it is a bit of radionic history that may have gone unsung had the picture not come into my possession. The picture though not too clear nevertheless coincides exactly with the description given, the lower aspects of the buttocks can be seen and the back of the thighs. Hovering at the left gluteal crease is the ball of light surrounding an elongated brighter light, which again contains an even brighter sphere of light. Above it to the left is the belt buckle. The casual tone of the description given by these two intrepid ladies who actually got radionic photographs from what must have been a simple and cheaply designed outfit amazes me. What baffles me is why they could see no practical value in it, and I wince to think they tore it all apart. Who knows what may have come out of this effort if it had been thoroughly investigated.

Today with the vast strides being made in energy field photography pioneered by the Kirlians in Russia, many people are being forced to acknowledge the evidence that auras or corona discharges as they are sometimes called do exist. Obviously the aura as seen by the clairvoyant has not yet been photographed by these new techniques, but the first steps have been taken, and it can only be a matter of time before this is accomplished. Where radionic photography will fit into this exploration of the bio-psychic dimensions of man remains to be seen. There are many imponderables that need to be clarified, not least amongst them the problem of getting consistent reactions between the operator, the film and the radionic camera. At present the inconsistent results that are obtained have proved to be a source of some discouragement, and so too no doubt is the fact that science can turn its back on twelve thousand very remarkable pictures, and dismiss them as a fraud because they do not fit into the narrow framework of present day scientific knowledge.

Given the time, given the money, given a properly structured research programme and a group of people who have the capacity to sensitize film, and who can work from a combined esoteric and scientific basis, I think that radionic photography as a tool for exploring the ether fields, as a diagnostic scanner of the human aura, would come to the fore. Its possibilities and range are virtually unlimited.

Surely such a programme will some day materialize and we shall see whole series of pictures that even science cannot ignore.

Chapter Five

RADIONIC POTENTIZING – REMEDIES FROM THE ETHER-FIELD

'This is the property of our medicine into which the previous body of the spirits are reduced: that, at first, one part thereof shall tinge ten parts of this perfect body: then one hundred, then a thousand and so on infinitely on . . . and by how much more often the medicine is dissolved, by so much the more it is increased in virtue.'

Hermes Trismigestus

The thought that it might be possible to utilize the energy fields we live in to impregnate or charge a carrier substance with healing forces, is one that has caught the imagination of many people. If as Ruth Drown suggests that the vibrations of everything in the world are always present at any given point, and that we have only to draw these vibrations from the Life-field in order to apply them for healing purposes, then there is more than a distinct possibility that remedies can be drawn from the formative forces, held in a carrier substance to be later given to patients as indicated.

Edwin Babbitt who won world fame for his theories and healing work with colour in the late 1800's, found that it was possible to charge water or granulated sugar of milk with the chemical healing properties of colour. His technique was to use a chromo-lense which was a rather flat flask-like glass container. Normally these were used to pass light through in order to treat patients directly with the colour the lense happened to be. In order to charge water or milk sugar with blue for instance, he would take a blue lense, fill it with the carrier substance and allow the lense to hang in a window or by exposing it to sunlight. This he claimed charged the substance with an immense amount of medicinal power, enough in fact to make hundreds of doses at a time.

In his book *The Principles of Light and Color* Babbitt makes mention of a substance called Od-sugar which had been devised by a Dr

50

von Gerhardt of Germany, and was found to have remarkable success as a curative agent. Od-sugar or Odo-magnetic sugar as it was sometimes called derived its name apparently from the odic force of Reichenbach. It consisted of sugar of milk that had been charged by certain rays of the sun through a prism. Babbitt, not too keen on the labelling of these charged sugars changed them from 'positive odo-magnetic sugar' and 'negative odo-magnetic sugar' to thermo-od-sugar and electro-od-sugar respectively. It seemed that the terms positive and negative with respect to the warm and cool ends of the spectrum of sunlight rather offended his sensibility.

Clearly Edwin Babbitt and Dr von Gerhardt were able to impregnate neutral carriers with healing energies, Babbitt himself is not slow to claim many cures based on treatment with these medicines. It is interesting to note that the medicines absorbed healing power through the action of sunlight and colour. Both doctors speak of the odic force, an energy that is common to all things having a special relationship to the forces flowing from the sun, which the Vedas would refer to as prana, Wilhelm Reich would call it orgone, the energy that fills all space and vitalizes all form.

Colour and the life sustaining healing energies of the sun are mentioned in the Chhandogya-Upanishad.

'Orange, blue, yellow, red, are not less in man's arteries than in the sun.
As a long highway passes between two villages, one at either end, so the sun's rays pass between this world and the (subtle) world beyond. They flow from the sun, enter into the arteries, flow back from the arteries, enter into the sun.'

Although the language is one of poetry the essence expressed merits our attention, or for that matter the attention of anyone who concerns himself with healing. Here the Indian sages are saying that the spectrum of life giving, healing colours or energies are to be found in both sun and man, and that there is a continual flow of this primal energy passing from the sun to the physical form, into the nadis or etheric nervous system of man and back out to the sun. In the extract I have cited, the term artery is used, this signifies the nadis or etheric web underlying the human form, not the arteries of the circulatory system as we know it. Surely it is not beyond the ingenuity of man to use these energies that Nature has so discreetly placed at his disposal.

Dr A. K. Bhattacharyya of India who has a large tele-therapy clinic in West Bengal uses two methods to transfer healing energies to carrier substances. In India where use is made of precious and semi-precious stones, one mode of preparation is to take a gem, say a ruby or an emerald, place it in a bottle containing an alcohol solution and leave this bottle in a dark container for approximately one month. At the end of that time the solution is impregnated with the radiations given off by the gems, medicines are then prepared from the solution. Another technique used at the clinic is to charge milk-sugar tablets by placing them in a container and exposing them to the radiations given off by gems that vibrate on the cone of a speaker unit, or are spun on discs attached to small electric motors. Judging from the results obtained from using medicines prepared in this way, there is clearly a transfer of energies taking place, and this energy can be taken up by the patient's body in order to eliminate disease.

Here in England the Bach Flower Remedies are prepared in a way that transfers the vibratory healing qualities of the blooms to a liquid carrier substance, in this case pure stream water. There are two methods of preparing these remedies. One is the sun method, used for the flowers that bloom during the late spring and in the summer when the power of the radiations from the sun hit the earth with full intensity. Then there is the boiling method utilizing flowers and twigs of the trees and plants and bushes that bloom earlier in the year.

To prepare remedies by the sun method the flowers are picked around 9 am, when the blooms are freshly opened. They are then placed in glass bowls filled with stream water, which are stood near to the plants from which the blooms come. The blossoms float freely on the surface of the water which should be covered by them. No shadows should fall across the floating blossoms, and at no time should the water be touched by hand. They are left like this in the sun for three hours. At the end of this period the water is fully impregnated with the healing properties of the blooms. The vitalized water is placed in bottles and a little brandy is added to preserve the remedy.

To prepare remedies by the boiling method the blooms and twigs are gathered as for the sun method, placed in a saucepan and boiled gently for half an hour. The resulting liquid is filtered off and bottled with a measure of brandy. Here of course it is obvious that boiling the plant material will serve to extract these factors which act as healing agents, this is a technique which has been used for thousands of years and is more mechanical in nature than the sun method of floating where most subtle exchanges of energy occur naturally.

In both cases this stage of preparation is called the Essence. From the Essence a Stock bottle can be prepared by filling a one ounce bottle with brandy and adding two drops of Essence to it. The healing frequencies are retained indefinitely in the Stock preparation. To prepare a remedy for the patient, two drops from the Stock bottle are placed in one ounce of cold water to which is added one teaspoonful of brandy to keep the water clear. This remedy may now be taken internally; used as a lotion or a teaspoonful placed in a bath for bathing. Which ever way it is used the highly diluted healing qualities of the plants still retain their power to bring balance to the force fields of man, particularly those of the astral and mental levels.

There is another rather unusual preparation which utilizes the healing forces to be found in plants; this comes from Nairn in Scotland and is called Exultation of Flowers. This preparation is made by a Mr Alick McInnes who describes it as 'Electrical impulses in stable suspension, obtained by potentizing the following flowers by an entirely new method and in harmony with cosmic radiations'. I'll not go on to list the flowers that are used for there are some fifty-two of them.

When Mr McInnes speaks of potentizing he is not using the term in the homoeopathic sense, but he uses it to speak of the natural power or strength radiating from the blooms. After a great deal of experimental work Mr McInnes has found that he can transfer the healing power of each bloom to water without in any way damaging the plant. Each flower, he says, has wave-lengths or radiations which can be identified by anyone sensitive enough to register their impact. Some flowers give off circular radiations, others go from left to right or up and down or vice versa, some flow diagonally, some feel cold, others warm.

These radiations can be transferred to water when they are at full power, which varies from plant to plant, and under the right conditions this transfer is instantaneous, and it is claimed that the water used can actually be seen to change. At first sight the technique may seem a bit odd. There is Mr McInnes, bowl of water in hand, moving it rhythmically in front of the blooms who's healing radiations he wants to capture. He says it is possible to pick up with your own body the sensation of the energy transferring itself to the water where it is held indefinitely.

A year ago I would have been a trifle sceptical about this claim, but since working with Dr Marcel Vogel in man-plant communication experiments, I have for myself had direct experience of this type of phenomena. The plant in this case was the split-leaf philodendron – in order to come into resonance with the plant for the purposes of experimentation, it is necessary to go through the process known as 'charging the plant'. This is done by moving the flat hand over the leaf at a distance of a few inches in a circular movement. Then the hand is moved up and down over the leaf until the power of its force-field is registered. The sensation is one of a drawing power, which when very strong may cause the fingers to ache. I have seen Marcel Vogel do this to a Diffenbachia plant with his hand a foot away from the leaf, moving it very gently to the sensed rhythm of the plant's force-field, until every leaf moved up and down and the plant looked as though it were about to take off and fly. If I passed my hand through the intervening space between his hand and the leaf, an electric like shock ran through my finger tips. After such experiences I am prepared to believe that Mr McInnes is on to something. He says himself, that if more people took the time to try and tune into these radiations coming from plants, they too would experience them, and I am sure he is right. Most of us are quick to dismiss something like this without really taking the time out to test the theory.

Only certain combinations of flower radiations can be used in Exultation of Flowers, as it has been found that some radiations cancel out others, others disturb the tempo of the mixture and exactly the same amount of each must be used to create a harmonious balance. What Mr McInnes says he is striving for is 'dead calm at the centre', the power of the calm at the centre of a cyclone. This force is analogous to the energies that are to be found in Exultation of Flowers, that will bring about a centre of calm in the patient allowing nature to restore health.

On the cover of the introductory booklet entitled 'Exultation of Flowers' is a coloured photograph of a Flowering Stock which having been treated with the flower preparation, had bloomed since July. The picture was taken on Christmas day and the plant was in full bloom, this, up in Scotland. Clearly visible in the picture, are as Mr McInnes points out, what appear to be ultra-violet rays and other bluish colourations on the rocks. Wilhelm Reich in his writings said that this colouration in photographs was the orgone energy and he illustrates it with two pictures, one of a vacuum tube filled with orgone in the laboratory, the other of a bear wallow. Both have the bluish overtones which can be seen in the photograph of the stock. There is I think a very close connection with orgone or pranic energies from the sun and these potentized mixtures of blooms.

Many people have asked Mr McInnes to prepare individual flowers for certain diseases, but he declines on the basis that it is more worthwhile to work from the concept that all sickness has a common cause, and that by striving to create a preparation that will eliminate that cause the end result will be infinitely more rewarding. Exultation of Flowers is not then, a specific for the treatment of any diagnosable disease, but is aimed at raising the vital forces in the human form to such a balance that they will offset the disease present. There can of course be no side effects from this preparation.

Exultation of Flowers has been in use for over sixteen years and is equally effective in the treatment of humans, plants or livestock. Its balance and its power to readjust individual needs, says Mr McInnes, is delicate, accurate and unfailing. Its action is entirely beneficial and in time removes symptoms that have been very deep-seated and of long standing.

Harkening back to earlier times at the beginning of this century, a book appeared entitled *Psychology of Botany-Minerals and Precious Stones*. It was written by a famous clairvoyant and astrologer who called himself Charubel. He claims in this book that trees, plants, mosses, precious and semi-precious stones and metals all had healing properties which could be tapped without actually taking the plant, stone or metal and making a preparation from it.

The technique was to simply stand near the tree or plant, mentally link up with it and draw upon the healing energies present. These energies could be used for one's own benefit or mentally directed to a patient. This flow of energies could be seen clairvoyantly by Charubel who describes them in his book, now unfortunately out of print. Obviously this method has drawbacks, not least amongst them the findings of the plant, stone or metal and the vagaries of inclement weather. Few healers I am sure would care to stand out in the forest on a wet day beaming healing energies to their patients. Charubel clearly forsaw this problem and found by dint of experimentation that through the clear mental visualization of a geometric pattern and the use of a mantram, he could draw upon the healing energy of the plant represented by that pattern and then direct it to the patient at a distance. We shall see soon how modern radionic potentizing uses the concept that a pattern or ratio can represent the healing force of any plant or substance known to have healing properties and that these healing forces can be radionically impregnated into a carrier substance.

Dr Ruth Drown it appears was the first radionic practitioner on record to prepare homoeopathic remedies by radionic means. Homoeopathic remedies above the potency of 12c have no measurable amount of the original substance left in them, probably not even a single atom. The dilution at this point is referred to as ultra-Avogadrian and is pure energy released from the substance that has been under preparation. She reasoned that if a homoeopathic remedy was in essence a form of pure healing energy, then she, through the use of her radionic instruments and the appropriate dial settings could draw that energy pattern from the ethers and use it to impregnate sac lac tablets.

In her instruction book for the use of the Drown Homo Vibra Ray

radionic instrument, she outlines the following method for remedy preparation under the heading:
METHOD OF PREPARING SPECIFIC REMEDIES USING SUGAR OF MILK TABLETS.

It is suggested that the operator get any potency desired from the homoeopathic pharmacy, free from alcohol if possible, and also procure some sugar of milk pellets, dry. In the specimen container of the instrument, place a vial of the remedy to be used for potentizing the plain sugar of milk pellets. Turn all the dials to zero. Begin with zero on the master dial, going upward until a reaction is obtained on the detector. Proceed with the second dial likewise; then the third, and so on until all the dials on the instrument have been used in the same way. Write this rate in a book opposite the name of the remedy and keep for future use. Now place on the foot-plates a small piece of block tin of the type used for the treatment electrodes, bent in the shape of a container. In this container place the sugar of milk (sac lac) pellets and fasten it to the foot-plates with the treatment cord. Leave the instrument set at the rate of the remedy and potentize until the sugar of milk pellets register a 'stick' (reaction from detector plate) when the remedy is removed from the specimen container.

Give the radio-potentized pellets to the patient, six of the small pellets, or three of the large size, every two hours the first day; every four hours the second day, and so on until there is an interval of twelve hours between doses. Then change the potency of the pellets to the next higher degree, and so on until the condition is eliminated. We find that many individuals lack certain cell salt vibrations which can be supplied in this way, thus hastening the healing.

Thus the concept that homoeopathic remedies could literally be manufactured by tapping their energy patterns in the ethers was made practical.

The Drown rates for the twelve tissue salts are as follows and can of course be used on any radionic instrument that uses a zero to ten ratio on the dials.

Calc. Fluor.	0–3–8–8	Kali Sulph.	0–3–1–8
Calc. Phos.	0–5–5–4	Mag. Phos.	0–4–3–8
Calc. Sulph.	0–7–7–3	Natrum Mur.	0–2–8–2
Ferrum Phos.	0–4–3–6	Natrum Phos.	0–3–5–6
Kali Mur.	0–3–2–7	Natrum Sulph.	0–4–7–6
Kali Phos.	0–5–2–8	Silicea.	0–3–6–3

During the early 1950's the De La Warr Laboratories in forwarding the work of Abrams and Drown, carried out, apart from the work of designing new instruments and developing diagnostic and treatment procedures, a certain amount of experimentation in methods of radionic potentization. Plants grown in inert substances but watered with liquid that had been potentized with the frequencies of various fertilizers, grew as though they had a full compliment of rich soil to bury their roots in. Mice were placed on vitamin C free diets. Separated into two groups, one lot were given water that had been radionically potentized with the rate of vitamin C and the others were given plain water to drink. Needless to say those that had the potentized water did not develop scurvy, those that were denied this and given plain water did get the disease. Experiments were also carried out in the radionic preparation of homoeopathic remedies which proved singularly successful.

Today the De La Warr Laboratories produce a very sophisticated electrically energized radionic diagnostic instrument which is also designed for potentizing. This instrument has twelve dials, a hand operated detector unit and is fitted with an oscillator which covers the frequency range from 9Hz to 1.1 mHz. The oscillator is transistorized and draws its power from an internally fitted battery, so the whole unit remains very portable and independent of mains electricity. The model which is used for potentizing work is slightly modified being fitted with an amplifier module to drive electro-magnetic energizing coils, these coils surround the specimen wells of the instrument. In order to make a potency for example of a homoeopathic remedy, the mother tincture of the remedy required is placed in one well, the rate representing the substance is put up on the dials and the frequency of the substance, determined radionically, is set on the oscillator. Plain, unmedicated sac lac tablets, water or an alcohol solution are placed in the other well. The instrument is switched on and this enables the operator to subject any substance, to quote the laboratory's description, to weak magnetic fields which are inimitable with other substances and this operation provides the phenomenon of potentization for the production of remedies. In other words the unmedicated tablets become impregnated with a potentisation of the tincture in the other well, this transfer takes about twenty minutes to accomplish.

The man who has probably done the most work along these lines using the de la Warr equipment, is a Dr Poul Goos, PhD of the Radionisk Laboratorium in Denmark. He is assisted in his work by Walter Egger, a micro-chemical engineer who is also a skilled homoeopath. They felt, like Drown, that there was an affinity between radionics and homoeopathy because both are more concerned with the energy aspect of things than the material. They felt it was worth experimenting to see if radionic rates could be impregnated into an alcohol solution. Dr Goos recalls the first experiment with these words.

'Using the Mark VII instrument we set the radionic dials for the rate of "heart" (5238). We then took a small bottle containing 60% alcohol which we placed in the well between the magnets and rotated it until we found the critical position. Using the measuring dial we tried to find if there was any reaction but there was none. After half an hour, however, there was indeed a reaction and, turning the measuring dial slowly, we found a reaction at 5. We had therefore obtained a reaction of 5 radionic units (100 being the maximum) which we called Delawarr Units, written DLW.

We then continued for another half hour and again measured, but this time detected an emanation of 12 DLW. After two hours we managed to obtain a reaction of 30 DLW and after that it did not rise further.'

A further 24 hours in the instrument, recalls Dr Goos did not in any way alter this reading. It seemed that the solution had taken up all it could of that particular frequency. Dr Goos and his assistant went on to run many more experiments and they found that by impregnating an alcohol solution with the healing frequencies needed by a patient, they could then administer drops of this liquid morning and evening, and this oral ingestion seemed to enhance the radionic treatment at a distance.

They then experimented with polypharmacy, that is the mixing of different remedies, in their case radionic rates, into one solution. This too worked and it was found that if this solution was placed in a container on the radionic treatment instrument along with the patient's blood spot, that a whole series of rates or healing frequencies could be delivered, so to speak, at one time.

Dr Goos has gone on to develop a liquid mixture containing 222 different rates. This preparation he calls SOMAVITAL and he uses it to treat his patients both radionically and orally, to this of course he adds whatever individual rates each patient may need. Other experimental work has shown that it is possible to take a homoeopathic remedy which has been prepared by standard methods at the pharmacy, and through the radionic instrument transfer the pattern of the remedy to plain unmedicated sac lac tablets. It then carries the original power to heal itself and without diminishing the energy patterns of the pharmacy prepared tablets.

If rates or ratios could be impregnated into an alcohol solution and used for healing purposes, then the way was open to experiment with homoeopathic remedies. Dr Goos recalls his initial experiments in the following words.

'The next question to solve was this: Could we also potentize with the frequences emanating from the different homeopathic preparations? In my laboratory we have 172 different preparations, but of course, we did not know the radionic rates for each remedy, i.e. the figures we would have to set on the different dials of the instrument to achieve a frequency that matched the emanation of the homeopathic preparation. We therefore had to use another method to approach this problem and we did it in the following way:-

Let us suppose that we have a patient with a clinically manifested colitis and we have measured the radionic strength of the disease, to be for instance 40 DLW. In our homeopathetic books we then found the preparations which are active against this disease, and while we had the blood specimen of the patient in the well of the Diagnostic Instrument we placed a drop of the homeopathic preparation on the remedy plate and measured again; this measurement gave a reaction still at 40 DLW, – i.e. there was no effect from this preparation. We then tried another, a third, and so on; and let us assume that we found one or more preparations, each having an effect on the disease, so that we got reactions at for instance 20 DLW for one of them, while another still more effective would give a reaction at say 10 or 21 DLW.

If we placed these effective preparations all together on the remedy plate, we might reduce the reactions for colitis to as low as 3–4 DLW – or maybe even down to zero. The preparations having been selected in this way we now tried to use them to potentize a bottle of alcohol. Placing all the dials of the instrument on zero and placing the alcohol bottle in the well we also placed the new homeopathic preparation on the remedy plate and then rotated both of them separately, i.e. until we got a reaction that they were now placed in their "critical position". Let us assume again that this effect on the disease and with which we now wish to potentize the alcohol. We then left the bottle and the preparation on the instrument for 2 hours as usual and then tested whether the homeopathic frequencies had been transferred to the alcohol.

This we did in the following way:- We placed the blood specimen of the patient in the well, set the dials for colitis and got a reaction when we turned the measuring dial clockwise to 40 DLW. We then placed the alcohol bottle on the remedy plate, found the critical position, and measured again – and it was a pleasant surprise to notice that we got the reaction for colitis at 20 DLW, thus achieving an effect on the disease exactly similar to the one we had determined when we chose the preparations. In other words, the frequencies emanating from the preparation had in fact been transferred to the alcohol. This was a considerable result and naturally we proceeded and tried to transfer the frequencies of the other homeopathic preparations – which had proven effective – to the alcohol. The final result was that with the blood specimen of the patient in the well and the alcohol bottle on the remedy plate we achieved an effect upon the disease. We could now measure only a strength of the disease at 3 or 4 DLW or even zero DLW, just as we had found before placing all the effective homeopathic preparations together on the remedy plate. We concluded, therefore, that it was possible to transfer the emanation of the homeopathic preparations to the alcohol in the small bottle, and every experiment up to now – i.e. for more than a year – has shown the same result.'

At about the time these potentizing experiments were being carried out in Denmark, one of Britain's leading researchers in the field of radionics, Malcolm Rae, was applying his mind to the problems of radionic potentization of homoeopathic remedies with a view to simplifying and making the process more effective.

It has been established beyond any doubt as far as radionic practitioners and a growing number of doctors are concerned, that it is possible to make remedies that are effective by radionic means. The problem was to simplify and refine the techniques and the instrumentation. After a prodigious number of man-hours spent in experimentation, the running of exhaustive tests in the field, in discussion with doctors and radionic practitioners, there has emerged from the fertile and very practical mind of Malcolm Rae the answers to the simplification and increased effectiveness of both techniques and instrumentation for radionic potentization of remedies.

Rae felt that the standard radionic procedure to make homoeopathic remedies had a number of disadvantages, which had to be overcome. First the instrument itself is bulky, measuring perhaps 16″ by 28″ when open, some sets are of course smaller. Then there is always the problem of human error in setting up a number of rates on the dials to represent the remedy being made. On top of this is the time factor required to get maximum impregnation is a disadvantage, to some, so too is the fact that there is no way of immediately knowing when a certain potency or strength has been reached in the potentizing process.

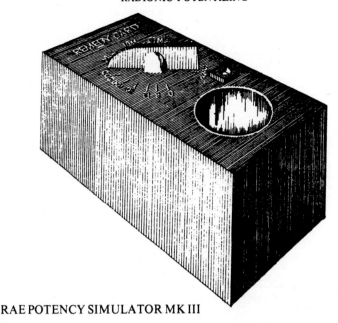

RAE POTENCY SIMULATOR MK III

Through persistent and careful research, Rae has overcome all of the above listed disadvantages. Firstly the Rae Potency Simulator Mk III instrument is very compact, measuring approximately 6″ long by 3″ wide and 2¼″ deep. The only setting required is that of the potency of remedy that is needed, these settings are clearly marked for the following potencies 6c, 12c, 30c, 100c, 200c, M, 10M, 50M, CM, MM and 10MM. Rae has found that control of potency can be achieved through the use of a proportional divider in the form of a radio potentiometer, and the calibrations enable the practitioner to select the potency he needs with accuracy. The points between the calibrations may also be used to make intermediate potencies.

Instead of setting up a series of rates to represent the remedy required, which is a somewhat complicated and time consuming act, Rae uses Simulator Cards. Each card is the geometric representation of a substance which can be used to make a homoeopathic remedy, thus a homoeopathic remedy which may have had a rate running into seven or eight numbers under the old system, is now represented by an accurate pattern or ratio on a card. These cards measuring about 2″ by 3″ have a pattern that consists of a series of concentric circles; there is a point at the centre and the remedy substance is represented by a series of partial radii, drawn from the inner circle towards the central point. A remedy may have up to six partial radii, and as Rae points out that the combinations of six radii drawn to an accuracy of 1° of arc, amount to 467, 916, 713, 911, 200, it will be a long, long time before a shortage of representational space occurs.

CORALLIUM RUBRUM   LYCOPODIUM CLAVATUM

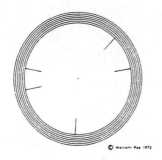 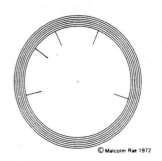

REMEDY SIMULATOR CARDS

The cards are of course designed to reproduce a substitute for any conventionally prepared remedy. To do this the card representing the remedy required is placed in the slot at the top of the instrument marked Remedy Card. The name of the remedy is always clearly visible above the surface panel, once again an advantage over rates set on dials. Next the potency is selected from the marked calibrations by turning the indicator to the strength required. In front of the potency selector is the well, this contains a fixed metal sleeve into which slides a crystalline plastic container, this can be taken out or left in as desired. If one wishes to potentize sac lac tablets they are first moistened with an alcohol solution and then placed in the well of the instrument or into a container bottle which can be put into the well. It takes 6 minutes to energize the tablets; if an alcohol solution is put into a bottle in the well the time to potentize this liquid is 1 minute, quite a difference to the two hours taken by the earlier experimenters.

The Rae Potency Simulator energizes and impregnates the carrier substance, be it sac lac, alcohol solution or water, through the introduction of the pattern which is magnetically energized within the instrument. If the pattern is withdrawn the substance in the well is immediately neutralized.

In an article which appeared in the March 1973 Radionic Quarterly, Rae listed the advantages of potency simulation in the following manner.

1 Consistency of remedies: All remedies made from any given card will possess identical characteristics.
2 Purity of remedies: The geometric pattern on the remedy card is drawn to represent the remedy in its perfect state: it cannot become contaminated during manufacture by the addition of traces of substances from which the manufacturing apparatus is constructed and its "perfect State" will exclude, in the cases of vegetable remedies, all variations which might result in succession-prepared remedies from differences in soil and other conditions of growth.
3 Speed: It requires no longer to prepare a remedy of MM potency than to prepare one of 30c. In either case only one minute is required if water is the medium potentized, and six minutes if sac lac is used. This, of course has special advantages when a high potency is required from a substance from which one has not been previously prepared.
4 Economy: If any remedy may be prepared within minutes, there is no reason for a practitioner to carry a large and comprehensive stock representing considerable frozen capital.
5 Versatility: If a substance possesses an exact definition, a card may be prepared from which remedies may be made, regardless of whether the substance itself is available to the manufacturing chemist, or indeed, whether it has ever been isolated. For example potencies made to represent gases and other substances not readily amenable to the succussion method, thus greatly extending the range of remedies.

Many homoeopathic practitioners carry a stock of remedies, and this stock over the years tends to increase as various potencies of each remedy are required and not all are used. There is of course an inevitable accumulation of remedies, some may be used up and have to be replenished at the pharmacy, but there is always this growing accumulation of remedies in those potencies which are not so frequently used. This stock of course represents a considerable investment of money which remains so to speak, tied up, as long as the remedies remain in stock.

Rae's latest development called, rather aptly, the Potency Preparer, will to my mind have a direct appeal to those many practitioners who carry a stock of remedies.

This instrument is slightly larger than the Potency Simulator but still very compact and easy to carry around. It looks somewhat similar but the casing is made of wood and it has two wells separated by the calibrated dial for potency selection. The entire instrument is magnetically energized and works in the following manner.

The Potency Preparer does not use cards like the simulator, but will prepare, within a few minutes, any desired potency from any material sample, or from any other potency of substance. The potency of the remedy required is set up on the calibrated dial, unmedicated sac lac tablets, water or an alcohol solution are placed in one well, and the substance or remedy from which a potency is required is placed in the other well. This permits potencies to be prepared from:

1   A patient's blood, urine, saliva, etc., for use in auto-therapy.
2   Samples of allopathic drugs when it is desirable to treat the patient to reduce their side effects.
3   Individual allergens, such as hair from a particular animal.
4   Gems. Minerals. Colours.
5   Any homoeopathic remedy or herbal remedy.

Once a potency has been made from an original substance, any other

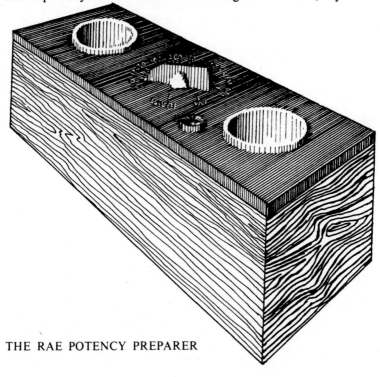

THE RAE POTENCY PREPARER

potency, higher or lower, may be made from it. It may therefore be used, as previously mentioned, to prepare different potencies from remedies which are already in stock. It is also an advantage that a group of remedies may be used to make a single potency of that grouping. These potencies should be thought of as information charged substances or message bearers that remind the patient's body what it needs to do in order to harmonize itself.

According to Rae when any substance is placed in the well of the instrument, its energy field is increased to 'maximum potency'. When it reaches this point the energy, which is a specific of the substance being potentized, like water, overflows as it were, and begins to seek its own level via the proportional divider or potency calibration dial. In other words a flow of the substance energy occurs between the well containing the 'maximum potency' energy field and the unmedicated tablets in the other well. This flow is of course controlled by the proportional divider which is set to the desired potency, thus the healing energies of any substance can be transferred to a carrier material and ultimately be used for treatment purposes.

There are some very distinct advantages to this method of potency preparation. Firstly any medical doctor who uses auto-therapy in his practice will be able to prepare remedies in a fraction of the time and with a fraction of effort compared to the standard method. There is also the advantage that any substance can be prepared in this way, quickly and simply and there is no need to keep a large stock of remedies of different potencies to hand.

I recall that my first reaction to the concept that one could potentize remedies literally out of the ethers, was one of scepticism. This was some four years ago, but I had an opportunity to borrow a Rae Mk II potency simulator from a friend who was going on holiday and this gave me a chance to test its efficacy.

Most of the time the instrument sat in my desk, but I had a patient who had come to me for a consultation regarding a low back problem, during the course of taking her case history I observed that all of the skin creases at the joints of her fingers were cracked open, some showing traces of blood. The condition, as you can imagine was a painful one and had not responded to any treatment over a period of many months. Prior to borrowing the simulator I had suggested she try certain homoeopathic medicines, unfortunately none of these seemed to help any more than the ointments given to her by her GP. So I decided to make up a remedy for her in the simulator. She took the tablets and within two weeks her hands had healed. Months later she phoned me to say the cracks were appearing again; by this time I did not have the simulator in my possession, so I resorted to standard pharmacy prepared remedies, but to no avail. Finally the patient said its no use, I want the kind of tablets you gave me that previously healed my hands. Now she had no way of knowing which remedies came from the simulator but she referred to them directly as the ones that had helped her. This was all rather an eye opener for me.

At about the same time I had a gentleman patient with a right sided sciatica. It had cleared once with conventional chiropractic treatment, and then the patient, who felled timber, lifted something in an awkward manner and the condition returned with a vengeance. Manipulation would not shift it so I made him a potency of Lycopodium in the simulator and within one day the sciatica had gone. He too had not responded to pharmacy prepared remedies.

Of course these are two isolated if rather dramatic cases and I was still not wholly convinced that the simulator really could produce remedies. A further two years elapsed before I began to use the Mk III potency simulator on a regular basis, and during this time I have spoken to medical doctors and practitioners in other healing disciplines who have related similar dramatic cures to me that they have observed from using simulated remedies and I feel that it is worth recording one or two of them here.

The first, a girl of seven weeks old, born the doctors said with a liver problem and jaundice. The condition was so acute that she was not given long to live. Exploratory surgery was suggested as the only hope. At this point she was treated with a combination of the following remedies made up in the simulator. Lycopodium, phytolacca, phosphorus, zinc and cuprum metallicum in solution form to be given as drops. Within one week the jaundice had completely cleared and the liver proceeded to function properly. The child now nine months old is a well and normal baby.

A boy, ten years of age suffering from muscular dystrophy, born with deformities of the hips, knees and feet. At the time of consultation he was suffering from acute polyarthritis and was in great pain. Phosphorus and zinc were potentized at 200c in solution form with the simulator and over a period of one week five doses of Calc. carb. 10mm. were similarly prepared and administered. There was a complete cessation of all pain within a week.

A man, sixty years old, suffering from angina pectoris and hypertension. Blood pressure at 240 over 170. Was given simulator prepared Crataegus Im. potency, two doses daily, this was later reduced to Crataegus 30c given three times daily. After six months his blood pressure stands at 146 over 92 and he can walk long distances which he had not been able to do prior to treatment.

The evidence seems to bear out that Ruth Drown who pioneered this field of potency simulation, was right when she said that it was possible by radionic means to tap the ether fields and to draw from them the energy patterns of any healing substance, and to impregnate that pattern into a suitable carrier material. It is a remarkable fact when all is said and done, and one worthy of careful contemplation for the implications are virtually unlimited.

Chapter Six

SCANNING THE HEALTH AURA

'The physician should speak of that which is invisible. What is visible should belong to his knowledge, and he should recognize the illnesses, just as everybody else who is not a physician, can recognize their symptoms. But this is far from making him a physician; he becomes a physician only when he knows that which is unnamed, invisible, and immaterial, yet efficacious.'

Paracelsus

When I first wrote *Radionics and the Subtle Anatomy of Man*, I stood firm in the conviction that the whole of radionic practice could be based upon the methods of analysis and treatment that I had outlined. I was sure that one could bypass the rather tedious task of analysing the states of the organic systems and go straight to the force centres in order to determine where health imbalances occurred. All of the early work I did along these lines tended to support this concept. Perhaps the high energy content of my initial enthusiasm carried all along with it, and this was supported by the good results obtained by practitioners who were using these techniques.

Gradually however I began to realize that where the early work in radionics had placed the emphasis upon the physical systems of man, and paid little attention to the subtle aspects, I had been equally guilty of putting all of the emphasis in the other direction, concerning myself with nothing but the subtle bodies and the chakras in particular. The first real inkling I had of this was when from time to time practitioners would come to me and relate that they were finding that they had to analyse at least some of the organic systems, as well as the chakras. Generally it surprised me and I tended to think that if they increased their knowledge of the structure and functioning of the subtle anatomy they really would not need to bother about the analysis of physical systems.

Practical experience has shown that for the time being at least, it is advantageous to combine the analysis of both the subtle bodies and the organic systems in order to get a clear picture as to just what is going on within a patient. There are probably any number of reasons for this, but I think that foremost amongst them is the fact that we have difficulty in relating to something as abstract as the subtle anatomy, whereas, on the other hand we have no such difficulty with the physical, it is something fundamental, visible, known to us and we can relate easily to it. This of course must enhance any linking that occurs between patient and practitioner for radionic healing purposes.

There is another factor too, which in order to grasp one must see, that although the chakras function as receivers and transmitters of energy, there are also energy transfers and imbalances occurring within the etheric body that do not necessarily involve the centres. To clarify this I am going to outline a case history that illustrates this point quite dramatically.

It concerns an individual who from time to time experienced periods of abdominal discomfort often coupled to symptoms of extreme fatigue, chest pains, difficulty in breathing accompanied by a feeling of numbness in the hands. At times these symptoms were so acute that the patient simply had to go to bed. Various blood tests were run and the heart was thoroughly checked: all clinical tests were negative.

A radionic analysis of the chakras revealed a well balanced system with the exception of the ajna which was slightly underactive and the base chakra which was overactive. The latter was probably in this state because it was attempting to pour in energy to offset the fatigue problem. Neither the ajna or base centre imbalances have any direct or apparent relationship to the symptom pattern of the patient. If in the normal course of events I had ignored the physical systems and treated the base centre to heal this patient, I would have missed the real cause of the trouble. (See figure overleaf.)

The diagnostic chart of the centres is a good illustration of just how one can miss factors if one focuses upon them to the exclusion of the organic systems. There is nothing there to really indicate the cause of this patient's distress.

DEVIATIONS FROM PERFECT STRUCTURE AND FUNCTIONING OF THE CHAKRAS:

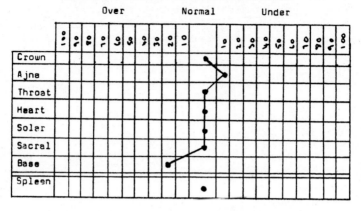

	Over										Normal	Under									
	100	90	80	70	60	50	40	30	20	10		10	20	30	40	50	60	70	80	90	100
Crown										●											
Ajna									●												
Throat										●											
Heart										●											
Solar										●											
Sacral									●												
Base								●													
Spleen											●										

If however we look at an analysis of the organ systems a clear picture begins to emerge. The method here used is the one devised by Malcolm Rae and the chart rather nicely illustrates a concept to be covered in the next chapter, that of expansion and contraction of the organism. The zero line near the periphery of the chart indicates the full expansiveness of the healthy state. The point of 100 degrees of deviation from perfect structure and functioning is the maximum contraction, this is at the edge of the circle in the middle of the chart. Any part of the organism that has a deviation close to the 100 mark is clearly in a bad state.

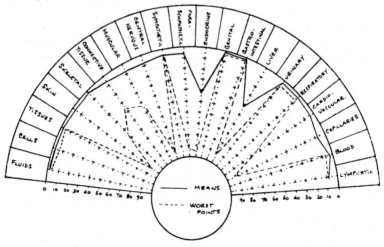

In order to keep things visually clear the readings on each organ system have been outlined in chart form rather than placing them around the outside of the chart as is done in practice. First the 'Worst Points' indicate the worst degree of imbalance in that system, it may be only a few cells. This case is an interesting example where the 'worst point' of the skin is 90·3 but the 'Mean' reading which represents the overall imbalance of the system as a whole is very low at 2·4 thus indicating that apart from a relatively small area the patient's skin is in good shape. This person had in fact at the time of the analysis a bad herpes simplex sore on the lower lip, hence the high reading of imbalance for the 'worst point'. The third reading is the 'worst point' following a one minute radionic treatment utilizing the potency simulator connected to a magnetic field interruptor. A special ratio card is used for this purpose. This one minute treatment has the effect, as Rae puts it, of 'skimming off the froth' and revealing those areas which should be of real concern to the practitioner. The readings on the nervous system frequently change dramatically with this treatment. This is clear from the case we are considering.

	Worst Point	Mean Reading	Worst Point After First Projection
Fluids	4·3	1·4	0
Cells	6·2	1·4	0
Tissues	4·4	1·3	0
Skin	90·3	2·4	7·2
Skeletal	50·5	2·3	3·5
Connective Tissue	30·5	5·4	3·2
Muscular	40·3	5·7	7·2
Central N. S.	90·4	7·3	8·7
Sympathetic N. S.	8·7	6·4	2·6
Para-Sympathetic N. S.	90·4	5·5	5·6
Endocrine	90·5	40·3	60·5
Genital	3·2	2·3	0
Gastro-Intestinal	6·3	2·5	1·6
Liver	90·3	40·2	30·7
Urinary	6·2	1·3	2·3
Respiratory	6·3	2·3	0
Cardio-Vascular	60·6	4·3	6·6
Capillaries	90·4	7·5	60·5
Blood	6·5	2·7	0
Lymphatic	9·6	7·3	0

If one goes through these figures carefully a clear picture of the problem begins to emerge. The projection for one minute using a special ratio card in the simulator quite clearly shows those factors which are of prime importance in this case. The endocrine system, the liver and the capillaries. All of the other readings have moved substantially towards zero, some in fact have reached it. Now it must be made clear at this point that these readings do not represent changes in the physical systems of the patient, but simply an alteration of the energy fields of the organic systems towards health, thus indicating that the ratio card used is suitable for overall treatment of the patient, but that individual treatment must be given to those factors which will emerge from a further analysis of the problem.

Next the patient's symptoms were written down in the manner shown on p. 72 and a ratio or rate determined which represented these symptoms as a totality.

A careful check through the endocrinology texts revealed that chest pains, difficulty in breathing, acute fatigue and the curious sensation of numbness that came into the hands during these spells, were all typical of para-thyroid dysfunction. So here was a case where a sub-clinical diphtheriae infection was creating toxins that were directly causing an imbalance in the para-thyroid glands. The high reading of imbalance for the liver was due to the attempts of this organ to deal with the toxins given off by the bacterial invasion of the gastro-intestinal tract.

Treatment indicated was the homoeopathic remedy Haematoxylon or Logwood, three oral transducers or tablets made up in the potency simulator at a potency of 10mm, plus radionic projection of the same and the group treatment ratio using the simulator.

It is worth noting at this point that I had never heard of the remedy that was radionically indicated for this patient. But on looking up the findings on it I could not help but feel that it bore out the accuracy of the analysis. Haematoxylon is characterized by a sense of constriction, as if a bar lay across the chest. Painful sensations from abdomen to throat causing pain in the region of the heart with oppression and heart palpitations. In women it especially relates to pain in the hypogastrium. It never ceases to amaze me how accurately a remedy picture can tie in with a radionic analysis . . . this one even details the pain from abdomen to throat which is the exact path or energy link between the intestinal tract and the para-thyroids that the bacterial toxin was taking; thus creating chest pains and dysponea.

Radionic treatments using the potency simulator as a projector, plus the three 'oral transducers' cleared this condition within a very short period. As I recollect the only orthodox medical treatment that

Chest pains. Restriction in chest
Difficult breathing
Acute fatigue
Abdominal discomfort

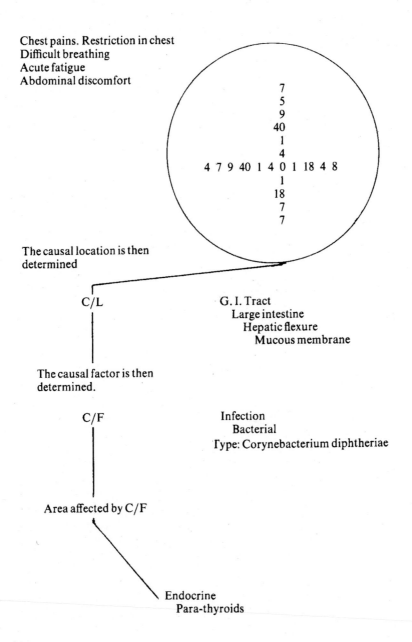

7
5
9
40
1
4
4 7 9 40 1 4 0 1 18 4 8
1
18
7
7

The causal location is then
determined

C/L   G. I. Tract
                    Large intestine
                       Hepatic flexure
                         Mucous membrane

The causal factor is then
determined.

C/F   Infection
                    Bacterial
             Type: Corynebacterium diphtheriae

Area affected by C/F

Endocrine
Para-thyroids

had been offered was Librium which was refused. I think that this case illustrates for us the need not only to look to the chakras but also to the organic systems of man if we are to do a thorough analysis of any health problem. This case clearly shows that an energy imbalance can create bad health without involving the centres, simply by disturbing the etheric body internally.

When Edward Russell, in his book *Report on Radionics*, summarized my work and Malcolm Rae's work in radionics, saying that he felt that there was a case for blending the two approaches. At the time I disagreed with him, but the wisdom of his insight has since become apparent and I find that a combination of our methods works admirably. The School of Radionics has also embraced this concept and students are now taught to analyse both the physical and subtle systems of man and to apply treatment on the basis of their findings.

The MK III Potency Simulator does make an interesting tool for radionic research and experimentation, this is clear from the case history outlined. Many practitioners plug it into their radionic diagnostic sets and in this way are able to add remedies to their broadcast treatments.

Modified and then attached to an interruptor, this instrument with a series of simulator cards representing various organ systems of the body, the endocrine glands, plus remedy cards and those representing hormones, colours and the atomic elements altogether make up a very compact radionic package that can be used to treat at a distance, and can be carried around very easily. I have personally used it in this way and find it most effective. Another method is to connect the simulator and interruptor to a modified de la Warr nine or twelve dial treatment instrument, or for that matter to any custom-built dial instrument. In this way, just as in using the diagnostic for treatment purposes, rates or ratios can be put up on the treatment set and the remedy, hormone, colour or whatever else is needed can be pulsed in from the simulator.

The use of an interruptor provides material for a variety of subjective experiments. The interruptor when it is switched on makes a clicking rather like a metronome but softer, the speed of this clicking can be speeded up or slowed down by turning a dial. When the appropriate card is placed in the simulator and the patient's sample is in the well of the instrument, I switch the interruptor on so that it clicks with a slow pulsating rhythm. Then sitting quietly with my eyes closed I visualize the 'line of light' connecting the patient with his sample in the instrument, and I see this line of light with a pulsing intensity which passes between the simulator and the patient, rather like the energy display on the tube of an oscilloscope. This intense blob of light that pulses along the line of light, I visualize to contain the healing frequency needed by the patient, and I see it fed into his energy fields in a steady stream of pulsations that coincide with the action of the interruptor. This is of course a subjective type of experiment but it does a number of things. First I believe it increases the effectiveness of the treatment, secondly it provides an exercise of visualization which is of great value to the practitioner, and last but far from least there will arise from this practice a series of subjective experiences which will be of value to any practitioner who treats at a distance.

I will give one example of such an experience that has happened to me. I was following the technique as outlined above during the treatment of a patient, when quite suddenly and spontaneously the remedy card in the simulator appeared before my mind's eye. The seven circles that form part of the ratio pattern were covered by a very bright but soft light that appeared to sweep around in a clockwise fashion, whenever this sweep of light reached one of the partial radii, a burst of light literally fired down the radii to the centre of the pattern. It was fascinating to watch, especially as it had appeared so spontaneously. This continued for a number of sweeps and then the whole picture just disappeared.

This reminded me of the statement by Rudolf Steiner, who could 'see' the flow of the etheric formative forces, that these energies flow in from an infinite circular periphery of space towards a central point and then they return to the periphery again. Certainly the power and speed with which the light flashed down the radii of the simulator pattern card from the circles seemed, within the confines of the experiment, to mirror this observation of his. One may argue that what happened was purely imagination on my part, perhaps it was, but the phenomenon happened so strongly and so spontaneously that I am inclined to disagree that it was just imagination. One must not discount I am sure, the powerful influence exerted by the mandala-like pattern of the simulator card, which if visualized clearly can trigger off such subjective experiences as I have related, which ultimately may be of use to the healer who works through radionics.

For each and everyone there are bound to be different experiences, and of course no radionic practitioner can sit down and do this visualization exercise with every patient he is going to treat. However if the exercise is practiced regularly I am sure that ultimately it will result in a vastly improved capacity to scan the health aura of the patient and to balance the forces within it when treating at a distance.

It has not been my intention in this chapter to go into full details of radionic analysis methods but simply to relate the fact that I now feel that it is important to take into consideration both the subtle and physical systems of man; this provides a balanced form of diagnosis which will enable the practitioner to be of greater help and usefulness to his patients.

Chapter Seven

THE SPINE AND
RADIONIC THERAPY

'The subject of spinal therapeutics has received less attention from the medical profession than it deserves.'

Spondylotherapy.
Dr A. Abrams, AM, LL D, MD, FRMS

In this chapter I am going to deal with the spine and some of the radionic approaches that are used to treat malfunctions in this area of the body. It may be hard for a chiropractor or an osteopath to accept that subluxations of the spine can be corrected at a distance, as they usually need to be adjusted by physical measures. The fact is that not all spinal problems can be treated radionically and then of course there is need for more physical treatment; however, even in these cases radionics can be utilised as an adjunct to manipulative procedures.

I am not going to deal with the gross aspects of the spine with which we should all be familiar, but with the more esoteric nature of this most important part of our anatomy. The spine since time immemorial has played a part in religious symbolism, being the pathway along which the fiery energies of spiritual regeneration ascend from the realms of darkness below to those of light above. The ancient Egyptians spoke of it as the link between the upper and lower heaven representing a vital sustaining power.

Recognized as a central column of power, care of the spine naturally played a paramount role in the healing techniques applied by the priest-physicians in the temples of light. The ancient Chinese as well as the Bohemians and the Greeks also recognized the importance of manipulative therapy in restoring health. It took the dark ages and a Papal decree to outlaw surgery and manipulation as heresy, and manipulation only began to emerge towards the end of the nineteenth century when Andrew Still founded osteopathy, and Daniel Palmer, a man with a profound understanding of the principles underlying the ancient wisdom, founded chiropractic. The shadow of the Papal decree still hangs heavy over the orthodoxy of today, where there is scant recognition of the importance of the spine to the inner and outer life of man and ultimately to his health on all levels of his being.

The state of the spine and posture are synonymous. Right posture is emphasized in the Yoga sutras of Patanjali. The aspirant to wisdom heeds the implications of right posture and knows that in his meditation work the spine must be upright and balanced, for the spine and its posture reflect the state of the inner man on the mental and emotional levels of his being. The first hindrance to soul cognition that Patanjali lists is physical disability . . . the body should be free of pain, balanced, refined and purified before it can withstand and clearly register the impacts of the higher states of consciousness. Few would disagree that problems of the spine with their attendant pain and disability constitute a hindrance to the true practice of the inner life.

From a physiological point of view, poor posture sets up a vicious circle of impaired oxygenation of tissues and a lowering of muscular tone, resulting in lowered resistance to disease, a predisposition to scoliosis, anaemia, general ill health and chronic backache; in other words it prevents or hinders the proper flow of energies through the anatomy of man. A recent survey of all the school children in a large city here in Britain revealed that 35,000 of them had defects in their body mechanics. Ten years of research into posture by the Canadian Memorial College of Chiropractic have shown that less than 0.5% of the adult population has a perfect posture. These figures are of course indicative of the great inner stresses and lack of balance that man is experiencing today.

If one searches through the ancient wisdom it is possible to find many references to the spine. For example in his book *The Aurora*, the Christian mystic Jacob Boehme referred to the spine or rather its subtle counterpart when he wrote:

> 'Now this wheel hath seven wheels one in another, and one nave which fitteth itself to all seven wheels, and all the seven wheels turn on that one nave. . . .'

The nave he wrote of is the subtle spine in etheric matter and the wheels are the spinning vortices of energy along the spine which are the gateways of consciousness, or in Hindu terminology, the chakras. Each chakra or wheel is externalized on the physical plane in the form of nerve ganglia and plexuses and ultimately as one of the endocrine glands. As I have mentioned before John wrote of these force centres in Revelations and referred to them as the seven seals on the back of the Book of Life. The seven chakras are said to be reflections of seven great centres of consciousness located in the brain. These seven according to the ancient wisdom, function through the centres on the spine in much the same way that the Seven Spirits before the Throne of God function through the planetary bodies. The correct and balanced function of these seven major spinal chakras expresses itself in absolute perfect health on all levels of the individual.

The nave or subtle spine, according to the ancient teachings of India, is comprised of three streams of energy; these three streams provide the link between the soul and its shadow or lower self in the three worlds. There are three paths along the spine, the first the Hindus refer to as the Sushumna which is the central path representing the Father, Spirit or Will aspect of Divinity. Then the Pingala on the left representing the Mother, Matter or Intelligence aspect and on the right the Ida which is the Son, Soul or Love-Wisdom aspect. When seen in motion the Ida and Pingala appear to exchange places; this motion gives rise to two spirals of energy moving about a central column and is represented in the healing arts by the Caduces. Similarly the rod of initiation wielded by the Bodhisattva, or world teacher, consists of a central straight serpent with two others intertwined about it, thus symbolizing the three outpourings of Diety; the three worlds in which man is immersed, and the spinal column with its three channels. It is also reflected, not unexpectedly, in the pattern of the DNA double-helix.

One cannot separate the condition of the spine from the health of the individual; Hippocrates himself admonished his students to look to the spine when disease pervaded the body of a patient. In *A Treatise on Cosmic Fire* by Alice Bailey, the Tibetan teacher states that the physician of the future will concern himself with two basic factors when dealing with disease. One is to see that there is correct alignment of the spine, and this is important because the spine stands central, not only to man's physical body but to his spiritual development too. The other factor is to bring about decongestion of the spleen; these in order that the latent fires of the physical body may correctly blend with the solar fire or pranic energies from the sun as they enter the etheric body. The Tibetan goes on to say that revelations in the healing field will come when. . . .

'. . .the medical profession concentrates upon the preventive action, substituting sunshine, a vegetarian diet and the application of the laws of magnetic vibration and vitality for the present regimen of drugs and surgical operations. Then will come the time when finer and better human beings will manifest on earth. When also physicians learn the nature of the etheric body, and the work of the spleen as a focal point for pranic emanations, then sound principles and methods will be introduced that will do away with such diseases as tuberculosis, debility, malnutrition and diseases of the blood and of the kidneys. When doctors comprehend the effect of emotions upon the nervous system, they will turn their attention to the amelioration of environal conditions and will study the effects of the emotional currents upon the fluids of the body, and primarily upon the great nerve centres, and the spinal column. When the connection between the dense physical and subtler bodies is a fact established in medical circles, then the right treatment of lunacy, obsessions and wrong mental conditions will be better comprehended, and the results more successful; when the nature of the egoic or soul force is studied, and the function of the physical brain as the transmitter of soul intent is better comprehended, then the coordination of man's entire being will be studied, and illness, debility and diseases will be treated through the cause and not just through effect.'

Radionics is beginning by its very nature to look at man along the lines suggested above. It sees disease as energy imbalance and it knows that through the careful selection and use of energies it can heal those imbalances that occur in the energy bodies of man. Spinal problems can be approached in a number of ways radionically, those that follow are a selection of the most effective ways.

In the 1950's an aircraft planning engineer by the name of Darrell Butcher became deeply involved in radionics. One of the first things that he discovered was that he could not use the stick method of radionic diagnosis on an instrument, nor could he use a pendulum for this purpose. A lesser man would have probably given up at this point and dismissed radionics, but Darrell Butcher dug his heels in and began to seek other methods of detection. The result of his research was called 'The Meter', this beautifully designed instrument comprised a perspex housing which contained a finely balanced needle, the needle was held in position by a tiny magnet above it. Below the point of the suspended needle was a semicircular dial marked with numbers ... Zero at centre and to the right it was marked off in three sections −1 −2 −3 and each section was further divided into tenths. The same was repeated on the left but as +1 +2 +3.

For diagnostic purposes the patient's sample was placed in front of the meter, the needle was set at zero. Then Butcher would mentally go through the list of diseases or their rates; when he came to the disease or causative factor of the patient the needle would automatically swing off from the zero and give a reading. Only two or three of these meters were made and I feel very fortunate to own one, and at the same time rather frustrated that I cannot work it. Apart from Mrs Butcher I have yet to find anyone who is able to cause that needle to swing when doing a diagnosis, or for that matter just by concentrating upon it. Darrell Butcher had this remarkable ability to move such things with his mind. He devised a series of three cones which looked rather like a wind measurement device and they balanced on a needle point . . . at one time, at a distance of some thirty miles he mentally caused these cones to spin around, then he stopped them and reversed their movement. This was some twenty years ago before such phenomena had caught the attention of scientists.

Having devised his own diagnostic methods and instrumentation he then developed a number of treatment instruments. One was called the 'Straw Hat'; this was a finely balanced cone around the rim of which were placed certain healing ratios in the form of cards with holes punched in them. The patient's sample was placed near the edge of the cone which soon began to revolve, and it turned until the patient's sample came opposite to the healing ratio that individual needed. When it was finished with it the cone simply took off again and moved until another ratio was presented to the patient's sample. This instrument and another called 'The Strip' are no longer available or in use but the Peggoty is and it is about this instrument that I want to deal in relationship to spinal problems.

Butcher said that the knowledge he applied to radionics came from a book that he picked up on a second hand stall for 5p. In it, he said, was all the information anyone would need in this field of healing. What the book was no one knows, nor its subject matter, suffice to say that from it he got the concept that energy flowed downwards at right angles to the earth plane. From this came the design of the Peggoty instrument. I am going to illustrate the panel of the Peggoty so that what follows is clear. It consists of a white perspex panel approximately $6\frac{3}{4}''$ by $5\frac{1}{4}''$ divided by lines into 120 squares. Each square has a small hole in it to receive a black peg. The pegs, set in certain patterns represent healing rates, or as Butcher preferred to call them, healing messages.

His theory was that energy flowed directly downwards onto the panel and then across it to the patient sample which floats on a metal holder balanced on a needle. If the panel has no black pins in it then there is no 'message', but with the pins placed in the panel to represent the rates that were needed by the patient, the energy flow is altered in such a way as to be beneficial to the patient at a distance. Butcher himself used the rates of de la Warr or Dr Ruth Drown on this instrument.

The Peggoty instrument is used like any other radionic treatment set, with the one difference that the rates are not complimented. I have

THE PEGGOTY

The black pegs inserted into the platform of the instrument represent the healing ratio to correct a vertebral subluxation. The area at the front of the platform is used to hold the patient's sample. The three pegs to the left of it are spare ones which can come into use if a ratio used has ten digits.

given these details of the Peggoty because every practitioner I know, almost without exception, says that it is the most effective way of treating spinal problems.

It may help at this point to describe briefly a spinal subluxation. Such a condition is often labelled with the misnomer 'slipped disc', for the record there is no such condition as a 'slipped disc', it is an anatomical impossibility for a disc to slip. It may degenerate, it may come under uneven stress due to a mal-aligned vertebra or it may in rare cases herniate, but it cannot slip.

A spinal subluxation occurs when a vertebra remains fixed at a point along its normal range of movement, this of course can happen to any joint of the body, but the spine and the pelvis seem particularly prone. This fixation of the vertebra creates an intense point of irritation which results in pain and often immobility. Very frequently the surrounding ligaments are involved, they become hypotonic and as a result stretch beyond their normal range, this puts the sensory nerves that are found within the ligament under traction and once again pain is the result, pain that is often referred to other areas of the body. In the case of low back problems pain is referred down the legs or into the groin or lower abdominal areas. It is essential in cases of back trouble to check the state of the ligaments that may be involved, seldom is a back problem simply a matter of a subluxated vertebra or sacro-iliac joint.

The ligaments may be treated radionically, and I have found that certain combinations of remedies made up in the Potency Preparer are excellent in restoring tone to ligament structures. Such a method is of course very useful in an osteopathic or chiropractic practice, particularly where no radionic therapy is utilized. The following basic combination is one that I have found effective time and time again.

The following are placed in the input well of the Potency Preparer.

Manganese phytate.
B12 Vitamin.

These two in combination have a very profound effect on the ligaments, causing their tonus to normalize. To these I add potencies, usually in ampule form, of the following homoeopathic remedies.

Adrenal whole gland.
Arnica.
Cartilago.
Intervertebral disc.
Bamboo and/or Bamboo Disc.

I use adrenal whole gland because when ligaments are involved in a back problem, and they nearly always are, then this gland has a role to play. Stress is a major factor in back problems for this particular reason; adrenalin is released into the blood stream every time we come under stress, be it emotional or physical. We should run or fight to burn up this adrenalin, but normally we don't, so it remains in the blood stream. Now there are certain factors in adrenalin that inhibit the normal growth of maintenance cells in ligaments. When this occurs the ligament stretches, especially at points where it may have been weakened by falls or injuries in the past and the result is a back problem, often very acute and frequently arising for no apparent cause. Adrenal gland gives support by clearing out excessive amounts of adrenalin in the blood stream.

This then is the basic preparation; to this may be added other remedies that may be indicated, for example Rhus tox., Ruta, Bellis Perennis, Lycopodium or any other suitable remedy. I have also used the Potency Simulator to broadcast Manganese Phytate B12 and found it very effective in healing back problems as an adjunct to chiropractic treatment.

As I said at the beginning of this chapter it is sometimes hard to accept that spinal problems can be helped radionically, especially at a distance, so I would like to close with two very interesting quotations from the Agni Yoga books, *Brotherhood* and *Aum* which illustrate the sensitivity of the spine to directed thought. One states:

> 'Sometimes one may feel, as it were, vibratory contacts on the skin in various parts of the body, but most of all in the region of the spine; it should be understood that this manifestation is also connected with thought transmission, especially when thought of great tension is under way.'

The other:

> 'Thought is lightening. A received thought frequently strikes luminous manifestations within us; it then increases the radiance of the chakras. Likewise, it may be understood that spinal vibrations are closely connected with the reception of thought.'

Of course with spinal problems it is always best to check thoroughly if the patient is best served by physical manipulation, and if so refer them to a competent practitioner in this field. In treating spinal problems radionically it is essential to analyse carefully the state of the base and alta-major chakras for both of them govern the spine from different ends of the column and it is through these chakras that radionic treatment is best directed.

Chapter Eight

BIO-DYNAMIC RHYTHM

'Every particle of our body can be brought so absolutely into rhythm that nothing can go out of harmony.'

Spiritual Healing
Swami Paramananda

Now let us return to some further considerations arising from the Geometric Etheric Link hypothesis. As previously mentioned our knowledge of the relationship between man and the spectrum of surrounding and penetrating universal forces, small as it is, demands that in postulating a force field through which the radiesthetist works, such a field must be appropriate to the nature and behaviour of the protoplasmic cell. The hypothetical geometric etheric link would appear to provide the symbol of this force field and directly beg comparison to the configuration of the DNA double-helix, thus relating force field to protoplasmic cell.

Any hypothesis, if it is to have validity, must provide the key to a better understanding of the work from which it emerged. Inevitably, through such understanding, knowledge of a practical nature must accrue; which can express itself through improved diagnostic and therapeutic techniques. In radiesthesia and radionics we are concerned with restoring the dynamic balance of forces within the patient, and so the query arises: can the geometric link hypothesis provide us with a clue that will lead to a more efficient and basic approach to the eradication of biodynamic aberrations within the human form? I hope to show that it does just that.

There would appear to be a tendency among practitioners to think in terms of energies, radiations, force fields and so forth, and then diagnose and treat only in terms of organs and systems, this tends to complicate the practical nature of their work. Forget for a moment that man in his physical aspect is made up of flesh and bone, and think of him as a field of conditioned energies residing in a vast ocean of cosmic forces: think of him, in fact, as a cell within the Body of the Universe. Carry the analogy even further and stop to consider the relationship of a physical cell in the human form to the universe of cells in which it finds itself. The cell is in fact, like man, a unit of energy in a greater field of force.

The link hypothesis has led us to consider a universal force field containing a pattern of energies which may be utilized in contacting the patient for diagnostic and treatment purposes; and that in this force field is man himself, recognisable as a further complexity of energies containing the pattern of the double-helix, which in essence is a genetic formative force. At first sight this might not appear to provide us with any kind of a practical lead; however, the words, NATURE AND BEHAVIOUR OF THE PROTOPLASMIC CELL, from the opening paragraph, serve to synthesise several factors, namely ETHERIC LINKS—DNA—CELL— and PROTEIN. From the relationship of ideas conjured up by the association of these words we may derive something of value for our radionic work.

The normal biological state of the healthy protoplasmic cell is one of pulsating equilibrium, that is to say it contracts and expands within certain defined limits. This action is clearly seen during the successive phases of mitosis or cell division. The cell expands and in so doing rearranges its contents into various patterns. A rather interesting pattern occurs during the stage of cell division known as the metaphase. It is worth illustrating, particularly when one stops to consider that at this point the cell doubles its protein and nucleic acid content.

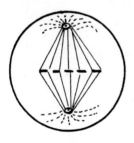 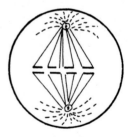

METAPHASE

After further rearrangement of the chromosomes, contraction occurs along the equatorial circumference of the cell and division is effected. It is important to remember that EXPANSION and CONTRACTION expresses the nature of the cell, and that these actions of the cell are the result of energy exchanges between it and the environment, both proximal and distal.

If the biological pulsation predominates in one direction or the other, a disturbance of equilibrium occurs. This block in plasma motility results in the reduction of the total energy function of the organism, creating a pre-disposition towards disease. For practical purposes in radionic analysis we may read it as follows:

Parasympathetics +	< Vital Force >	*Sympathetics* +
Expansion		Contraction
Relaxation		Tension and anxiety
Energies streaming from		Energies streaming from
centre to periphery		periphery to centre

The wisdom of Dr Guyon Richards is illustrated in his basing of remedies for organs and systems upon the positive and negative states of the sympathetic and parasympathetic nervous systems. Consciously or unconsciously he was dealing directly with the expansive and contractive states that occur within the human organism and find their expression in diseased tissues.

Contraction of the cell is concomitant with the contraction of the proteins which make up the cell, and there is no disease, illness or abnormality of the body that is not in some way related to protein metabolism. There are a number of factors which bring about contraction at a cellular level, foremost among them anxiety, a state in which the individual moves away from the world to the biological core of his being. Next in importance come the miasms and toxins which also play a large part in blocking plasmic motility and contracting the protein of the cells. Invariably there are a number of factors present in each case which create a contractive cell posture.

In treating a patient who suffers from a minimum of anxiety, and the major cause of plasmic contraction lies in a miasmic or toxic condition, the reaction to plasmic expansion due to the removal of the miasm or toxin will be minimal, and the patient will settle down to experience an improvement in health. On the other hand, where there is excessive anxiety the uncontrolled hyper-expansive phase due to the removal of the miasm may result in the triggering off of an anxiety state of no small proportions, for this reason: as soon as expansion occurs the patient is relating more directly to the ocean of life forces in which he lives (his energies are beginning to stream from the centre to the periphery) and such an experience can be overwhelming and terrifying to the neurotic. His polarity has been reversed and he will seek to contract to a point where he has only minimal contact with the unknown vastness of the life or vital force. This does raise the point as to who should be treated and cleared of miasms and toxins, and who should be left to work out his own destiny under the limits imposed upon him by The Law. Most of us have experienced the plaintive call of a patient who feels distinctly worse following radionic treatment; may it not be for the reason stated above?

Protein is necessary for every cell, tissue, organ and function of the human body. Protein molecules in the bloodstream are carrying agents for enzymes, fats, minerals, sugars, vitamins and hormones. Hormones are in fact protein in nature. The adrenals, pituitary and gonads unite protein molecules with other substances to form steroid hormones. The pancreas joins protein with zinc, the thyroid with iodine. Proteins, through the action of proteolytic agents and vitamin and mineral catalysts, are broken down into the amino acids which are assimilated through the intestinal wall and carried through the portal circulation to the liver. To our knowledge the body utilizes some twenty-six amino acids. Recognition of the importance of the state of the protein in the correct functioning of the human body and its vital role in the maintenance of health should make us stop to consider what part it might play as a therapeutic agent.

We know that the nucleic acid content of the cell doubles during the metaphase stage of mitotic division; we may therefore deduct that they play a role in the expansion of the cell. Now this suggests that as the protein of the cell expands following the removal of a miasm or toxin, that DNA and RNA in homoeopathic potencies may be used to control the rate of expansion and thus offset any unpleasant reactions on the part of the patient. All endocrine glands use protein in perfecting their secretions and we may observe that potentized amino acids have a regulatory effect upon the endocrine hierarchy whose major role is one of harmonizing the biodynamic forces of the body. The blood too is dependent upon correct protein balance if it is to be a carrier of the life force and here again the potentized amino acids can exert their healing power to restore harmony.

I believe that if the hypothesis of the geometric etheric link enables us to look upon the human organism in the light of force fields interacting rhythmically upon each other, and that health can be seen as a balancing of the expansive and contractive pulsation of the protoplasmic cell, then the concept has rendered a service. The application of potentized amino and nucleic acids may not be new to all of us, but to be aware of their capacity to control the negative reactions of overexpansion on a biodynamic level may serve to increase the efficacy of those measures we utilize daily in our radionic treatments. This is just one aspect opened through the use of the link as a symbol; the triangular relationship of energies may be applied to the esoteric anatomy of man and here one enters the realm of the reality behind the form and more advanced and subtle modes of therapy.

Chapter Nine

SOME ESOTERIC ASPECTS
OF RADIONICS

'The present age marvels at man's conquests of the forces of nature. Yet, this age of energy can only be triumphant when man can know and then direct and control the more important forces within himself.'

New Concepts in Diagnosis and Treatment
Dr Albert Abrams, AM, LLD, MD, FRMS.

Radionics occupies a rather curious and unique position in that as a healing art it represents a link between the more orthodox concepts of diagnosis and treatment and the realms of esoteric healing. It is a fact that some practitioners begin to work in the field of radionics, accepting that one can diagnose and treat at a distance but without realizing that there are any spiritual or philosophical implications at all in this work.

A doctor for example with a very orthodox background can use standard diagnostic procedures in radionics dealing only with the organic systems of man, and still with a minimum of effort feel that he is remaining close to the shoreline of his medical training and orthodox knowledge. Speak to him of subtle bodies and chakras and he would probably dismiss them as highly imaginative and irrelevant concepts. However the very act of taking up some form of radionic work indicates that he is, even if unconsciously, beginning to embrace a wider and more profound approach to healing, which in the fullness of time will lead him into more esoteric fields.

Few can work at radionics for any length of time without realizing the vast potential it represents, not only in terms of service to others, but in terms of an accelerated inner development and sensitivity. Clearly George de la Warr felt this when he wrote:

'Radionics is an etheric science and can, in fact, lead the way to a modern philosophy capable of correlating body with mind and therefore with Universal Mind.'

Let us consider this more fully. If a radionic analysis is to be done properly and with accuracy the practitioner must, with practice, develop the ability to align his mental and emotional bodies with the etheric vehicle. Alignment of the bodies means to bring them into a state of quiescent balance in which their vibratory qualities are synchronized. This allows a free and clear flow of information to reach the consciousness and physical brain of the practitioner. In other words he is in an alert, meditative state with his mind focused one-pointedly on the problem he has to scan, which in this case is the nature of any imbalances in the health aura of the patient. It takes no imagination to realize what effect this has on the practitioner, for the continual alignment of his lower-self must eventually lead to a vastly increased awareness.

Now let us take this a step further. In making a radionic analysis the practitioner is psychometrizing the blood spot or snippet of hair of the patient, and through this focused attention he is registering the state of the patient's health through his own systems. In other words he is getting a feedback through the ether field, or through the field of mind if you prefer to call it that, this tells him just what is wrong with the patient. To psychometrize means to touch and if we examine the esoteric meaning of the word touch we find that touch gives man an idea of relative quantity and enables him to fix his relative value as regards other bodies extraneous to himself. Touch is that innate recognition of contact through the use of the mind, so the practitioner touches with his mind the aura of the patient at a distance and is able to determine its qualities.

If we take the sense of touch and extend its nature into the subtle levels it can be seen to evolve in the following manner.

On the physical plane we have the physical sense of touch.

On the astral it becomes psychometry, on the mental level it evolves to planetary psychometry, on the buddhic plane it is healing and on the atmic plane, service. Service is the spontaneous release and flow of soul energy unencumbered by any traits of the low-self or personality.

Diagramatically we have this unfoldment of the sense of touch the development of which is greatly enhanced through the practice of radionics, because the motive is to serve others and not selfishly directed towards self-development. Through service to others our inner development unfolds naturally and rhythmically, there is no forcing through concern of one's own self which always creates imbalances which later have to be corrected.

ATMIC   ↑   Service

BUDDHIC	↑	Healing
MENTAL	↑	Planetary psychometry
ASTRAL	↑	Psychometry
PHYSICAL	↑	Touch

Radionics is of course concerned with two main factors in this list. The first is the psychic sense of touch or psychometry which is astral in nature, the other factor is healing which is related to the plane of the Christ or the Buddhic plane. Radionics is therefore an astral-buddhic healing technique. Now according to the esoteric teachings the first solar system which long ago went into dissolution, formed to establish mind and body, it was in effect a physical-mental solar system. The second solar system to be formed, in which we now live is in the process of unfolding and developing the feeling and love aspects of its nature. In other words we live in an astral-buddhic solar system. This is the Christ system in which the qualities of love and feeling are being developed and the second aspect of Deity is therefore predominant.

If we live in an astral-buddhic solar system and radionics is an astral-buddhic healing art, I cannot but feel that it must have a very profound value in the scheme of things. The following quotation from *Treatise on Cosmic Fire* if mediated upon will reveal just how important this work is.

'It is of value to study the extensions of physical plane touch on other planes and to see whither we are led. It is the faculty which enables us to arrive at the essence by due recognition of the veiling sheath. It enables the Thinker who fully utilizes it to put himself en rapport with the essence of all selves at all stages, and thereby aid in the due evolution of the sheath and actively to serve. A Lord of Compassion is one who (by means of touch) feels with, fully comprehends, and realises the manner in which to heal and correct the inadequacies of the not-self and thus actively to serve the plan of evolution. We should study likewise in this connection the value of touch as demonstrated by the healers of the race (those on the Bodhisattva line) and the effect of the Law of Attraction and Repulsion as thus manipulated by them. Students of etymology will have noted that the origin of the word touch is somewhat obscure, but probably means to 'draw with quick motion'. Herein lies the whole secret of this objective solar system, and herein will be demonstrated the quickening of vibration by means of touch. Inertia, mobility, rhythm are the qualities manifested by the not-self. Rhythm, Balance, and stable vibration are achieved by means of this very faculty of touch or feeling. Let me illustrate briefly so as to make the problem somewhat clearer. What results in meditation? By dint of strenuous effort and due attention to the rules laid down, the aspirant succeeds in touching matter of a quality rarer than is his usual custom. He contacts his causal body, in time he contacts the matter of the buddhic plane. By means of this touch his own vibration is temporarily and briefly quickened.'

When the veiling sheath is spoken of it refers to the lower bodies of mental, astral and etheric matter. The Thinker is the soul at its own level. If the above passage is read with care and reflected upon by the radionic practitioner he will begin to intuit his own role in the evolutionary scheme of things. I believe that the practice of radionics will one day be seen as a method of training which will lead the individual to function as part of certain groups, which in the Aquarian Age will have a definite service to perform. Radionics will be seen as the gateway to the practice of a far more profound way of healing. It is said that this applies to other areas of service. Take for example the fireman of our cities and towns. On the surface this appears to be a fairly mundane job, but it is said that by being trained to fight fires and learning all about the nature of fire the fireman is actually preparing for service which will come into effect thousands of years from now when man will have the need to be able to control the fire elementals from the higher levels of consciousness. In America today there are tribes of Indians who specialize in the fighting of fires and they are dropped by parachute into mountainous areas to carry out this task. Their capacity to control fire with an absolute minimum of equipment is legendary, obviously they have this ability in them to control fire elementals. Eventually man will of course find that they can be controlled from the levels of the higher mind.

Radio astronomers with all of their abstract mathematical knowledge, are in training along lines that will eventually enable them to work with the Lipika Lords or Lords of Karma. This is a very abstract subject and I do not intend to enlarge upon it here, but simply put it forward because it illustrates that every task or job of work we do, although it may seem pointless, mundane, perhaps boring in the extreme, is a means of inner growth and it will eventually lead to service of great importance to humanity. Radionics if we study it with care will clearly indicate along what lines and goals of service the practitioner is moving.

If one moves away from the standard practice of radionics which basically considers only the more orthodox factors such as the organic systems, then it becomes possible to relate radionics to more spiritual and philosophical factors. It leads us for example into the realms of Eastern thought and to consider the esoteric anatomy of man, this I have outlined in *Radionics and The Subtle Anatomy of Man*. If a practitioner begins to diagnose in terms of the chakras and subtle bodies it has the effect of sensitizing his own systems at these levels, it must always be remembered that 'Energy follows Thought' . . . if you diagnose the chakras and think in these terms, it will, as I have said, literally sensitize these systems in the practitioner. This has the effect of course, of pushing forward his own inner development in a balanced way. Eventually this will enable him to dispense with any form of radionic instrumentation, for he will through dint of hard work in the service of others come to know his own energy systems to be the finest healing instrument ever devised, one that can register the tiniest imbalance in the health of a patient, and as one that can consciously select and transmit the required healing energies.

This is not just a theoretical concept, there are practitioners who have reached this point and discarded their instruments; who can with precise mental action formulate the characteristics of a homoeopathic medicine for example, and mentally project it into a wasp sting so that there is no effect from that sting on the person who has been stung. In the case I am thinking of the sting did begin to have effect some hours later when the mentally projected treatment began to wear off. Further treatment caused it to disappear again. So you see the power of the mind is developed in radionics as well as the power to visualize clearly; both of these are of vital importance to anyone who is going to serve in the field of healing.

There is a rather fascinating passage from the *Psychology of Botany – Minerals and Precious Stones* by Charubel, which illustrates the method he used to mentally locate a healing plant that he required to use for distant treatment.

'One day a friend of mine was suddenly siezed with inward pains of a sharp pricking character in the lower part of the chest, extending down the left side. I was induced to place myself in a calm and tranquil condition – just as I am ever in the habit of doing, when in the quest of a correct vision of any person, subject or thing – saying to myself: "I will look into the vast field of nature", I have no crotchets, or preconceptions of my own to intercept from me the light of heaven, "I will look, yes, I will look. There must be a remedy for every ill, the plaster must be as large as the wound." Such was my faith at that time, such is my faith at this day; and, so far as my experience goes on, has carried me hitherto, there is every probability that the future will find me much in advance of what I am this day.

I had not wandered far, nor waited long, before I saw a bush covered with yellow bloom resting on green foliage. At first I took this bush to be the Broom, but on closer inspection I found it to be the Gorse-bush, as soon as I made this discovery I realized an aura emanating from the bush of a brown colour, I united this aura with an aura which enveloped my patient, and within a quarter of an hour the pain was gone. A short time after this I had taken a severe cold, with pain in the ear; this pain was gradually becoming more severe. I looked in the same way as before. I had not looked long before I saw the Maidenhair Fern, I manipulated the aura as before, and the pain in the left ear left me and did not return.

Another case was that of a young girl who was suffering from extreme weakness accompanied with a cough, which, as it appears was the sequel of Scarlatina. This patient resided at the time in Cornwall. I looked as in the other cases, and the humble Lichen appeared the aura of which was gray mingled with red. This I applied in a few successive days, suffice to say that she was cured in a week.'

These cases illustrate rather nicely the treatment of a patient who was present. The treatment of one's own self and treatment at a distance. It is clear that Charubel used the mind to scan the ethers for the required remedy, and through the ether field he united, by the power of his mind and its capacity to visualize, the aura of the plant and the aura of the patient. I am firmly convinced that any radionic treatment that incorporates the act of visualization in this manner will be far more effective than a rather hurried putting up of a healing rate on the treatment instrument. Both practitioner and patient would benefit from such a method applied to radionic work.

Although it is possible eventually to put radionic instruments to one side, it is important to use them for as long as they are needed, for their use provides a focal point for the practitioner to work through and they are a means to an end. It is no use jumping in the deep end and discarding instruments prematurely. By analogy we may consider an abstract impressionist artist such as Rothko or Jackson Pollock. Rothko painted the most beautiful blocks of subtle colour that seemed to float on the canvas. Pollock of course is well known for his action painting in which he literally threw and dribbled paint over huge canvases, producing some remarkable works which were later compared with, and appeared identical to high magnification pictures of brain cells. My point is that these two artists arrived at this point of expression through the hard and disciplined school of represensational art; without such a background their abstract art would not have had content or meaning. The same applies to radionics, it is essential to train and work in this field using the available instrumentation, through this the practitioner's inner 'instrumentation' is developed, and ultimately, like the artist he can discard the conventional and move into the realms of abstraction and the pure use of the higher mind.

APPENDICES A – B – C

FOR RADIONIC
PRACTITIONERS

APPENDIX A

Drown rates for use in potentizing with any radionic instrument that is calibrated 0 to 10.

Minerals

Radium	834300	Silver	8343880
Gold	834803	Platinum	834109
Lead	8341609	Cobalt	8346003
Aluminium	8349799	Sulphur	834446
Antimony	834909	Iron	834492
Manganese	83455	Silicon	83467
Phosphorus	834695	Tin	8341184
Iodine	834884	Carbon	83487
Sodium	83445	Zinc	8345009
Copper	83410837	Arsenic	8344999
Uranium	8349099	Potassium	83454
Magnesium	834871	Lime	8341753

Remedies

Aconitum	901558	Cocaine	901206
Belladonna	901448	Conium	9015239
Camphor	90180741		

Gases

Chlorine	6789301	Nitrogen	6789721
Hydrogen	6789169	Oxygen	6789263

APPENDIX B

Drown rates for use with the Peggoty instrument when treating spinal or other skeletal problems.

Conditions

Impinged nerves	90·63	Fractured ribs	90·7542
Strain	60·93865	Lumbar abscess	30·2987
Cord compression	90·192297	Trauma	10·92
Fracture of spine	90·784297	Arthritis (Rheum)	90·2
Sciatica	40·351935	Sacro-iliac disease	40·2854374
Displaced cartilage	40·35154	Nerve trunk	
Sprain of spinal col.	70·599279	pressure	50·11109279
Spondylitis	10·92297	Cervical rib	70·74694542
Lumbago	40·599193		

Bones

Elbow	84115	Right hip	84479
Ankle	841893	Left hip	84439
Toes	84422	Ilium	84374
Fingers	84895	Knee	84121
Thumbs	84891	Pelvis	84525
Ribs	84542	Scapula	84397
Sternum	84263	Periosteum	359

Vertebrae

Atlas	842823	Lumbar	84193
Cervical	84692	Sacral	84854
Dorsal	84183	Coccyx	84188

Joints

Ankle	8491892	Wrist	84910041
Knee	8493343	Finger	849950
Toe	849422	Mandible	8491736
Sacro-iliac	849923	Vertebral	849546
Hip	8491775	Shoulder	8493323

Elbows	84910043	Sterni-Clav.	849693
Costal-Vert.	849902	Costal-Sterni	849503
Coccygeal	849248		

Muscular   and   Ligamentous
Structures

Cartilages	154	Muscular system	37472
Ensiform cartilage	2382	Muscle	599
Rib cartilage	2356	Inter-costal muscle	356
Semilunar cartilage	9003	Involuntary muscle	59980
Fascia	104	Voluntary muscle	59918
Ligamentous system	2843	Tendons	645
Ligaments	854		

APPENDIX C

In chapter six mention was made of a special ratio card, this Appendix has been added in order that some details can be given that will be of use to radionic practitioners, especially those who have large or rapidly growing practices.

It is a fact that standard radionic treatment procedures can be notoriously time consuming, and unless the practitioner has an assistant, he or she can reach a point where a great amount of time has to be devoted to the existing practice, leaving little to deal with new patients. This difficulty frequently arises as a practice grows in size and the patient load increases.

This raises the question . . . Is it possible to treat effectively more patients in less time? Four years ago Malcolm Rae turned his mind to this problem and through his researches formulated the concept of the Comprehensive Therapy Ratio (CTR). The idea was that this ratio expressed on a card, should give a wide spectrum of corrective treatment to any patient at any time, and that it should in no way have any adverse effects. The card was to carry coded instructions to the patient, instructing him as an energy field, what to do in order to bring balance to the field and ultimately the physical form.

Now one cannot just sit down and devise a ratio that will encompass the corrective patterns for all diseases, superfluities or deficiencies in one fell swoop. It is a progressive, on-going process and Rae has now worked on this ratio pattern for four years. It has involved literally hundreds of hours of work in order to refine the pattern of the ratio card, continually building in new factors as they came to light. In the initial stages of this research, cards were frequently changed; today, having developed, used and ultimately discarded some 2,000 cards a stabilization has become very evident and alterations are infrequent.

There are a number of advantages in using this method of treatment, and I will discuss them in the order that they apply. First the card is used to project treatment directly after all 'mean' and 'worst 'point' readings have been made on the patient's systems. This has the effect as previously mentioned of 'skimming off the froth' and the following re-analysis of the 'worst points' leaves a clear indication of the *fundamental pattern of disorders* in the patient.

By using the CTR projection daily the practitioner has more time to devote to seeking out the specifics each patient may need in the way of oral remedies, homoeopathic medicines, tissue salts, vitamins or minerals. Or to search for any special radionic projections that may be needed. Experience has shown however that once the patient is being treated by CTR then seldom are other remedy or ratio projections needed and this certainly saves much time and energy for the practitioner. Oral remedies are of course prescribed from the appropriate source.

The Potency Simulator is used for these CTR projections. The Simulator can be fitted with a magnetic field interruptor and a timing switch. This is then wedded to a 35mm automatically operating slide projector. Patient samples are set into 35mm slide holders, placed in the slide tray, which should preferably have a circular form as it holds more slides and automatically comes back to the first one when all patient samples have come into proximity to the probe which projects the CTR energy.

In this way all patients are treated daily on an automatic basis, and Rae finds that for him this method is effective and it leaves him time to deal with new patients and any emergencies that may arise, not to mention further research into the expanding field of radionics.

SUGGESTED READING

The Chain of Life by DR GUYON RICHARDS. Health Science Press.

Forces and Fields by MARY HESSE, MSC., PHD. Littlefield Adams.

Galaxies of Life edited by DR S. KRIPPNER & D. RUBIN. Interface.

The Human Aura by DR W. J. KILNER. University Books.

Keeley and his Discoveries by C. BLOOMFIELD MOORE. University Books.

The Loom of Creation by DR DENNIS MILNER & E. SMART. Neville Spearman Ltd.

The Odic Force by KARL VON REICHENBACH. University Press.

The Pattern of Health by DR AUBREY WESTLAKE, Shambhala.

The Principles of Light and Colour by E. BABBITT. University Books.

Radionics and the Subtle Anatomy of Man by DAVID V. TANSLEY. Health Science Press.

Radionics, Radiesthesia and Physics by WILLIAM A. TILLER, PHD. This is available as an article from the Radionic Association.

Report on Radionics by EDWARD RUSSELL. Neville Spearman Ltd.

Telepathy and the Etheric Vehicle by ALICE BAILEY. Lucis Press.

For further information about radionics contact –

> The Secretary,
> The Radionic Association,
> Field House,
> Peaslake,
> Surrey.

For the MK III Potency Simulator and Potency Preparer –

> Electro Radiesthesia Consultants,
> 47 Lee High Road,
> Lewisham,
> London, S.E.13.

THE SACRAL PLEXUS REGION

This picture represents a vertical section of the lower abdominal area. The dark curved mass in the bottom left corner is a cross section of the sacrum. Above it the anterior portion of the lumber vertebral bodies are to be seen. The three dark tracks flowing from this area and converging at the top right-hand side of the picture are blood vessels in a state of diapedesis. The meningeal coccus infection upon which the Radio-Vision camera was tuned appear as myriads of tiny white dots which can be clearly seen in front of the lumbar vertebrae and throughout other areas of the photograph. The structure of the gluteal muscle appears as the swirling area in front of the sacrum.

The infection was detected first by the Drown radionic diagnostic instrument. Then the camera was tuned to the infection, using the rate established in the diagnostic proceedure. The patient was well over a mile away from the camera when the picture was taken.

Drown Laboratories
Radio-Vision Department.

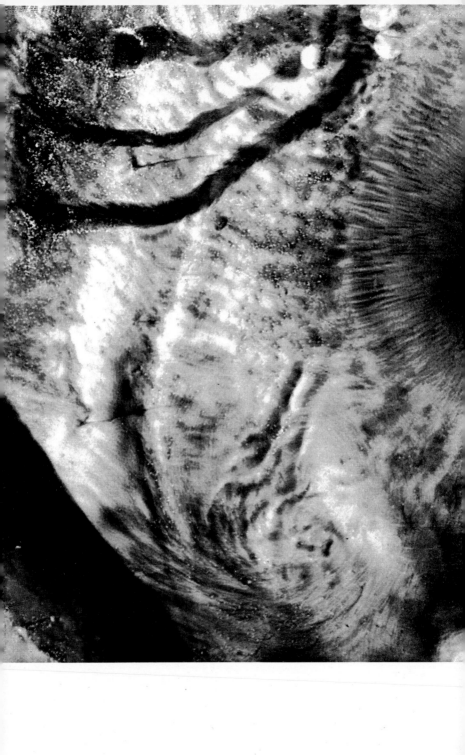

HYDATID CYST IN LIVER

Cross section of patient's liver, the picture being made from a blood-spot. Radionic diagnosis by Dr Drown recorded a hydatid cyst in the liver. The Radio-Vision camera was tuned to the cyst which appears as the dark area half way up on the right-hand side of the picture. The numerous white discs are cross sections of bile ducts and blood vessels.

The tissue structure in this picture should be compared with the one shown in PLATE THREE, also a picture of the liver.

Drown Laboratories
Radio-Vision Department.

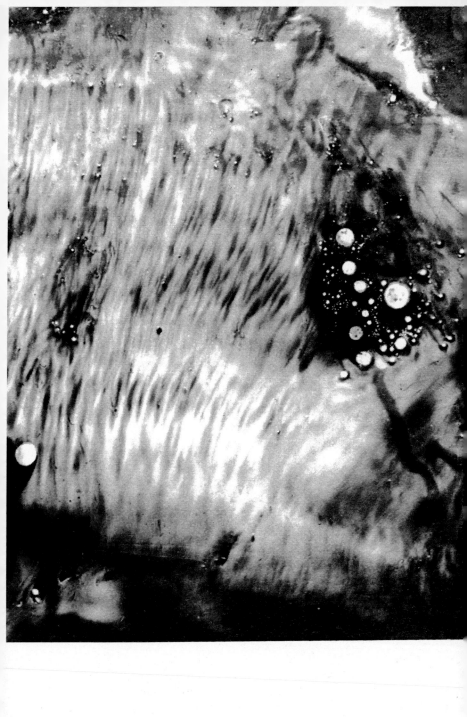

CANCER OF THE LIVER

This section of the liver shows cancer craters along the dark ridge which runs from the top left-hand area of the picture to half way down on the right. The craters appear as the lighter masses on this ridge.

What appears to be a vertically pointing crater with a light dot at its lower end, is in fact where a biopsy needle had been inserted into the liver in order to remove a sample for diagnostic purposes in a medical laboratory. The tissue structure is similar to that of the previous plate.

This picture was taken in Hollywood, California from a blood spot of the patient who was residing in Indiana.

Drown Laboratories
Radio-Vision Department.

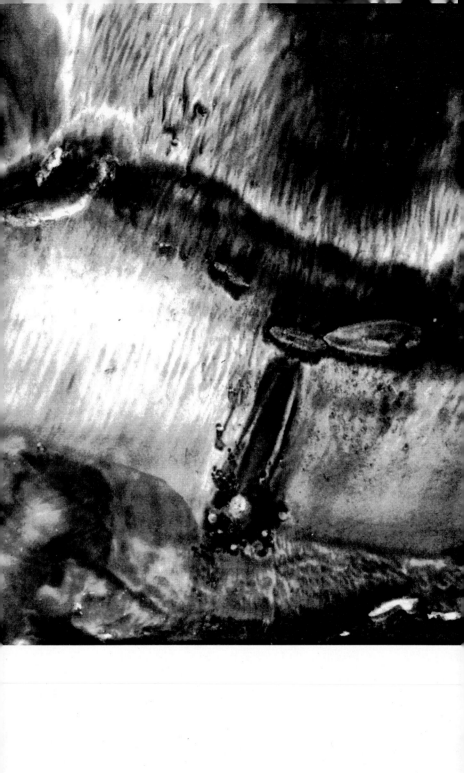

POST SURGICAL PICTURE – ABDOMEN

The line of the surgical incision runs from the centre of the bottom of the picture and upwards to the top right hand corner. The whitish effect along the line of incision is due to inflammation.

The clearly defined dark oblong areas running left from the incision are blood vessels severed during the operation.

Drown Laboratories
Radio-Vision Department.

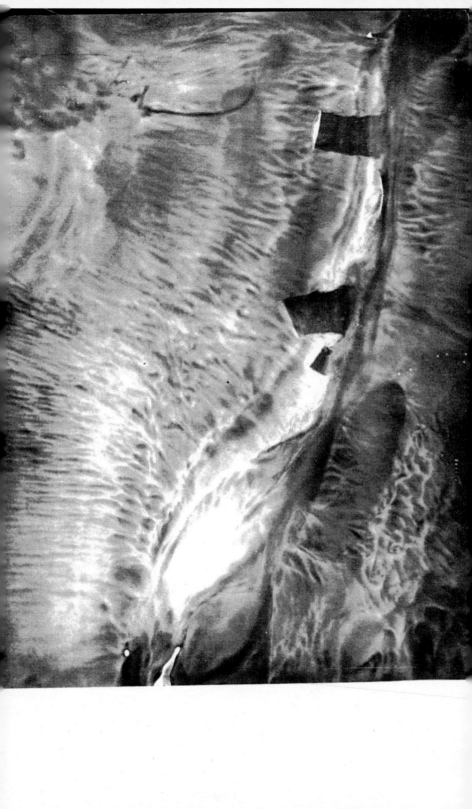

SURGICAL INSTRUMENTS PHOTOGRAPHED ACROSS 6,000 MILES

The patient, an English friend of Dr Drown's, wrote to her in 1950 that he was to have an operation for an ischio-rectal abscess. He asked Dr Drown to take a Radio-Vision picture before the operation, due the day following Dr Drown's receipt of his letter.

At 1 am the following morning Dr Drown tuned the camera to the man's abscess and this picture resulted. The outlines of two surgical instruments appear two thirds of the way up on the left-hand side of the photograph. The darker area above being the retractors and below them a pair of scissors, the pin holding the scissor blades together is clearly visible in the immediate region of the abscess.

Subsequent comparison of times showed that the patient was actually under surgery when the picture was being taken.

Drown Laboratories
Radio-Vision Department.

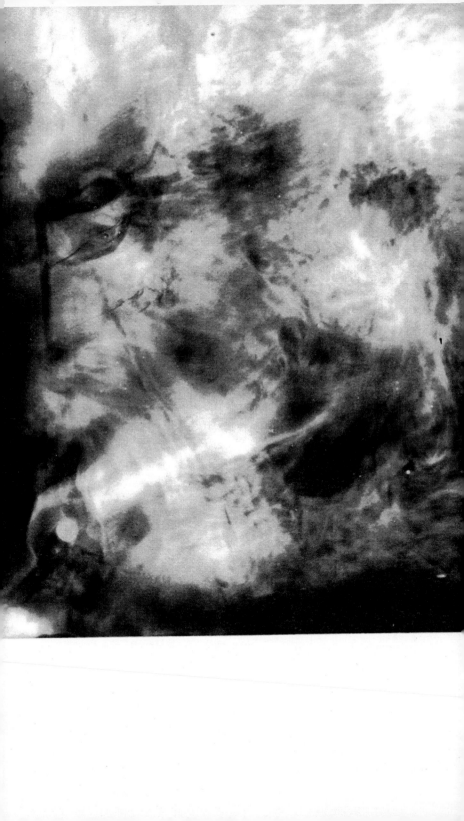

THE PINEAL GLAND

This radionic picture taken in the mid 1930's by Dr Drown from the blood-spot of a patient shows the pineal gland. It appears in the top left-hand section of the picture as a white mass surrounded by a not too clearly defined, darker aura. The gland according to Dr Drown is standing upright due to the fact that the picture was taken two weeks before the death of the individual concerned. This position, she reported, occurs in the new born baby and shortly before death.

Apart from the pineal gland the picture shows 'the light' in the brain which is spoken of in all esoteric literature and is frequently experienced during meditation, when it appears to flash suddenly through the ventricles of the brain. Ancient writers have stated, 'In the thalamus and pineal gland all things are comprehended.'

The lamina quadrigemina and cross sections of the third and fourth ventricles appear in the picture.

Drown Laboratories
Radio-Vision Department.

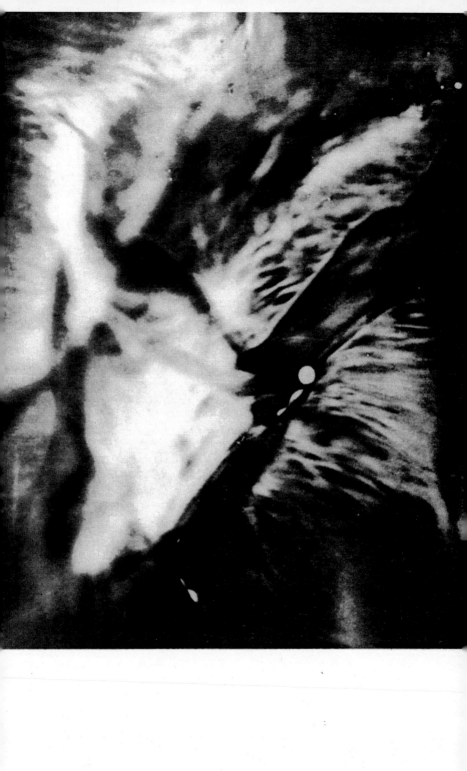

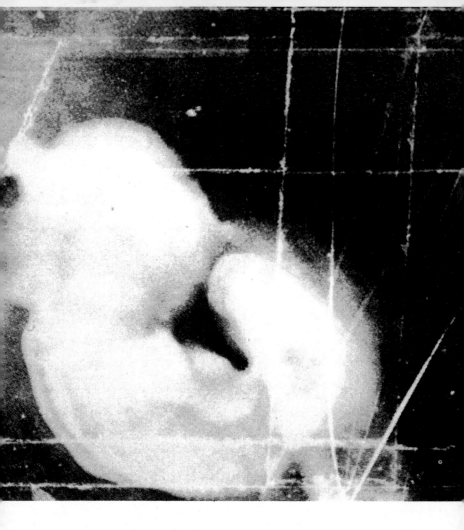

A most remarkable radionic photograph taken at the de la Warr laboratories with the camera tuned to a 3 month pregnancy. The foetus is clearly visible, yet the donor of the blood spot from which the photograph was taken was fifty four miles from the laboratory when the picture was taken.

Tuberculosis of the lungs. It is interesting to note that this patient only had one lung when the radionic picture was taken, yet two lungs show in this print. This is perhaps yet further evidence that it is the etheric lungs that have been filmed.

Radionic picture of a malignant tumor of the brain.

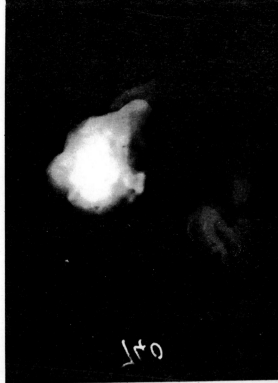

Pictures courtesy of Miss E. Baerlein & Mrs L. Dower.

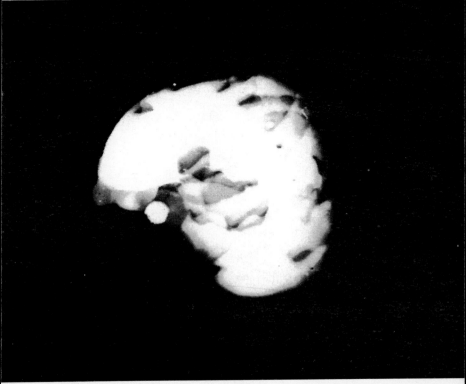

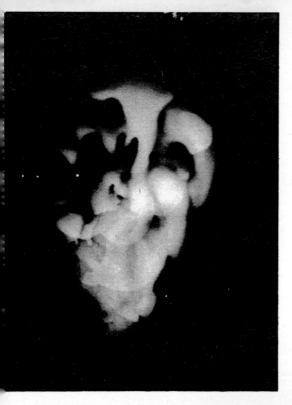

Radionic photograph of endocarditis.

Congestion of large intestine.

Courtesy of Miss E. Baerlein & Mrs L. Dower.

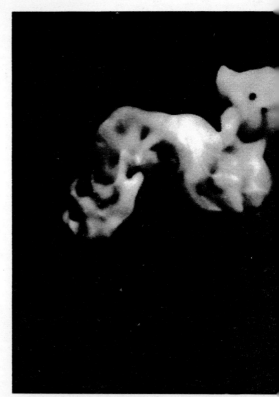

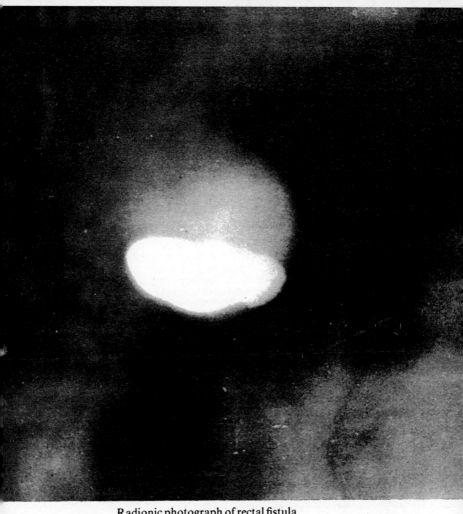

Radionic photograph of rectal fistula.

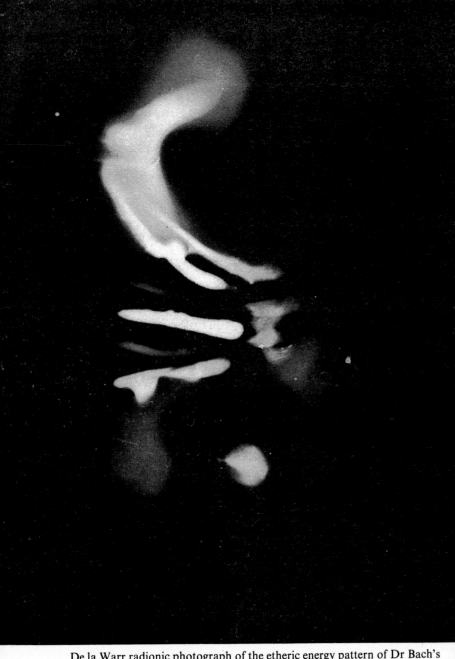

De la Warr radionic photograph of the etheric energy pattern of Dr Bach's Honeysuckle Remedy.